Class Piano Resource Materials

Level One

(Fifth Edition)

Compiled and edited by
W. Daniel Landes

Class Piano Resource Materials

© 2006, 2011 by Smith Creek Music
PO Box 140446
Nashville, TN 37214

www.smithcreekmusic.com
E-mail: info@smithcreekmusic.com

ISBN: 978-0-9835362-1-5

Introduction

These Class Piano Resource Materials were compiled for use in the secondary piano program at Belmont University, Nashville, TN. Consequently, the content has been shaped to a large extent by the various degree programs at that school and in particular, the Piano Proficiency Examination. Every school/department of music has some type of piano proficiency evaluation that music majors must past in order to complete their degree requirements. The various parts of the proficiency examination are the basic piano skills: repertory, scales and arpeggios, chords, harmonizing melodies, improvisation, transposition, etc. Consequently, the Class Piano Resource Materials are designed to prepare the student to pass a piano proficiency examination. Although intended for use in college classes, the materials are broad enough to be used in any class piano setting where there is a need for a graded series of books with a broad range of musical styles.

SCOPE OF THE MATERIALS

The Class Piano Resource Materials are arranged in five books by level of difficulty: Preparatory Level (no prior keyboard experience is assumed), Level One, Level Two, Level Three, and Level Four. Each level is organized according to specific goals that are spelled out clearly at the beginning of the book. Theory skills are not addressed in great detail because it is assumed that secondary piano classes are required in conjunction with the various theory classes such as Fundamentals of Music, Diatonic Harmony, etc. Detailed pedagogical information is outside the scope of these Resource Materials because it is believed that the instructor will give the necessary explanation of keyboard technique, theory, etc. Nevertheless, all the books in the various levels are organized in a more or less increasing level of difficulty if the instructor chooses to use them in that way. In addition, a suggested assignment schedule based on a 15-week semester is included in each level to aid the instructor in preparing weekly lesson plans.

DESCRIPTION OF THE MATERIALS

In selecting the materials, specific composers and periods of music were a strong factor. Each level contains representative repertory by classical composers such as Bach and Beethoven. Twentieth century classical music composers such as Bartók, Persichetti, and Schoenberg are included as well as representative pieces in various styles composed specifically for these books by the author and colleagues. Each level includes music in a popular style. These are not arrangements of popular tunes but are original compositions which appear here for the first time. It is hoped that the choice of repertory and other material will give the student a well-rounded musical experience and help develop keyboard and musicianship skills necessary for the professional musician.

INTEGRATION OF TECHNOLOGY

Each level (book) has an accompanying interactive computer application that been designed as an addition resource, including links to a WEB site. The application runs on Apple Macintosh computers using system OSX 10.2 and higher. Versions for Windows computers, IPads, etc. may be available in the future. Detailed information regarding the implementation of the computer software is available on the website:

www.smithcreekmusic.com

COPYRIGHTS

Every effort was made to contact the owners of copyrights for permission to make settings or use pieces. If mistakes have occurred, they will be corrected as soon as possible. Please email us at:

info@smithcreekmusic.com.

The author is grateful to the owners of copyrighted material who have granted permission to use their works. Where copyrighted material is used, a copyright notice appears at the bottom of the page.

Table of Contents

Page

SCALES, ARPEGGIOS & EXERCISES

APPENDIXES

For more resources, please visit the WEB SITE at:

www.smithcreekmusic.com

General Goals

(Level One)

1. Reinforce orientation to the keyboard:

   -- demonstrate an understanding of proper sitting position and hand position
   -- play in the correct octave
   -- demonstrate an understanding of basic hand positions: 5-finger hand positions, octave hand positions

2. Play major, natural minor, and harmonic minor scales in Group I (those scales in which the thumbs play together) in a steady tempo and with correct fingering.

3. Play assigned repertory pieces with acceptable proficiency.

4. Begin to demonstrate an understanding of the proper use of the sustain pedal by using it where indicated in assigned repertory.

5. Play major and minor triads on any note.

6. Play block-style cadences in major and minor keys through two accidentals.

7. Harmonize simple melodies using primary chords.

8. Improvise simple melodies (chord tones, passing tones, neighbor tones) over given chord progressions in major and minor keys through two accidentals.

9. Create simple improvised arrangements of familiar melodies.

10. Transpose a single line (treble or bass clef) up and down a half step and whole step.

11. Continue to develop concepts of sight reading:

12. Demonstrate the proper use of the sustain pedal.

13. Play simple technical exercises.

14. Continue to develop concepts of style and musicianship and demonstrate these in the performance of assigned repertory:

   -- expression
   -- articulation
   -- dynamics
   -- tempo

Class Notes

Little Dance

From *First Term at the Piano*, No. 8. Long and Short. Budapest, 1913

Invention

Annonymous
arr. WDL

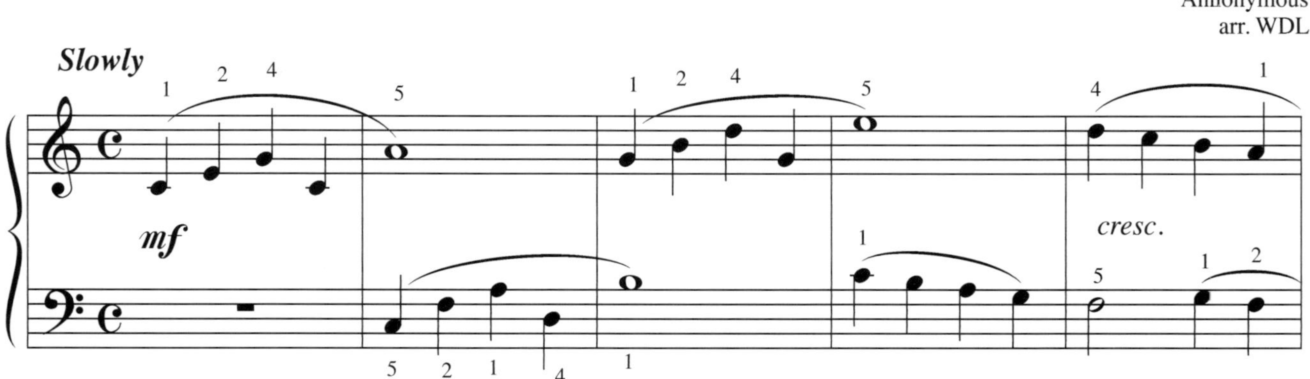

Romance

(Secondo)

Anton Diabelli, c. 1820

Romance
(Primo)

Anton Diabelli, c. 1820

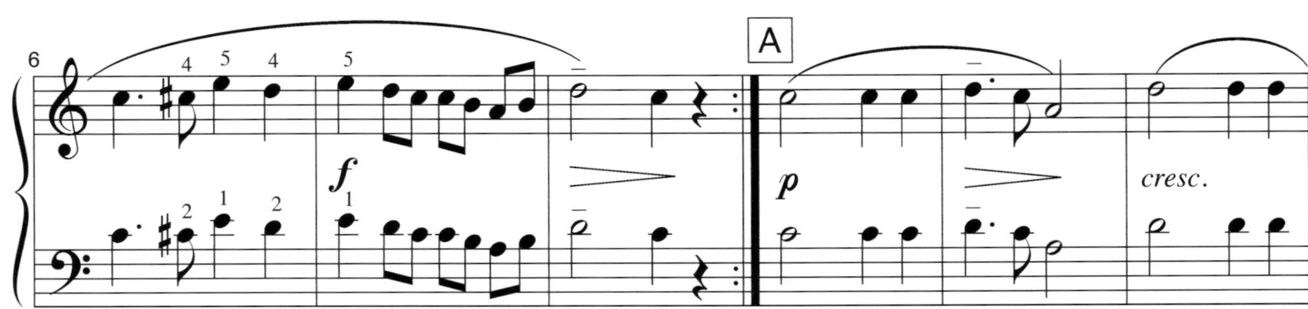

My Lord, What a Morning

Little Étude

From *First Term at the Piano*, No. 10. Folk Melody. Budapest, 1913

Round Dance

WDL

Triads, etc.

Bagpipes

WDL

Moderato

Folk Song

Béla Bartók. 1913

From *First Term at the Piano*, No. 15. Bedtime. Budapest, 1913

Tallis' Canon

Thomas Tallis
Arr. WDL

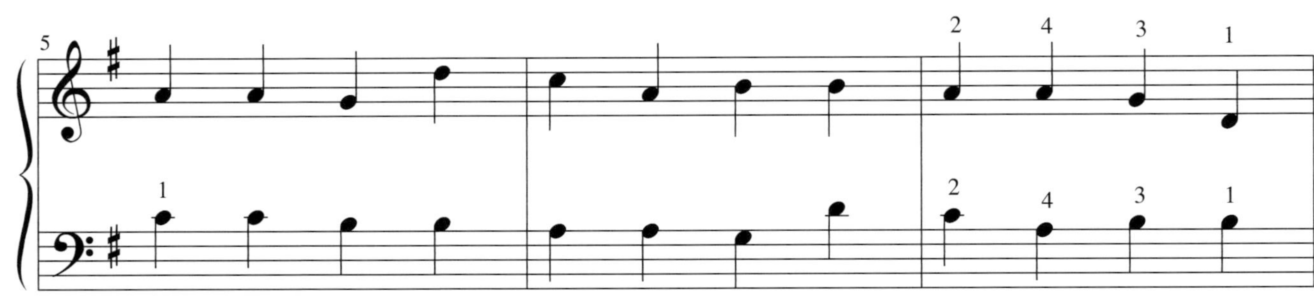

Minuet in F

From Leopold Mozart's Notebook

Minuet in C

Tischner
Arr. by WDL

Reflection

From *For Children, Book I*, No. 3. Former Friends, Budapest, 1909

Ninety-Fifth

Adapted from
Wyeth's, *Repository of Sacred Music, Part 2nd,*
1820

Peasant Song

From *Ten Easy Pieces*, No. 1. Peasant Song, Budapest, 1909

Uncle Willie Is Up to His Old Tricks Again

WDL

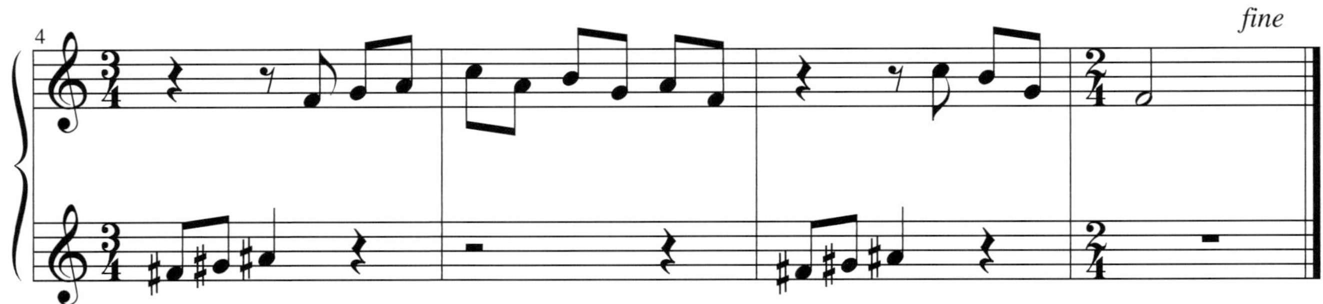

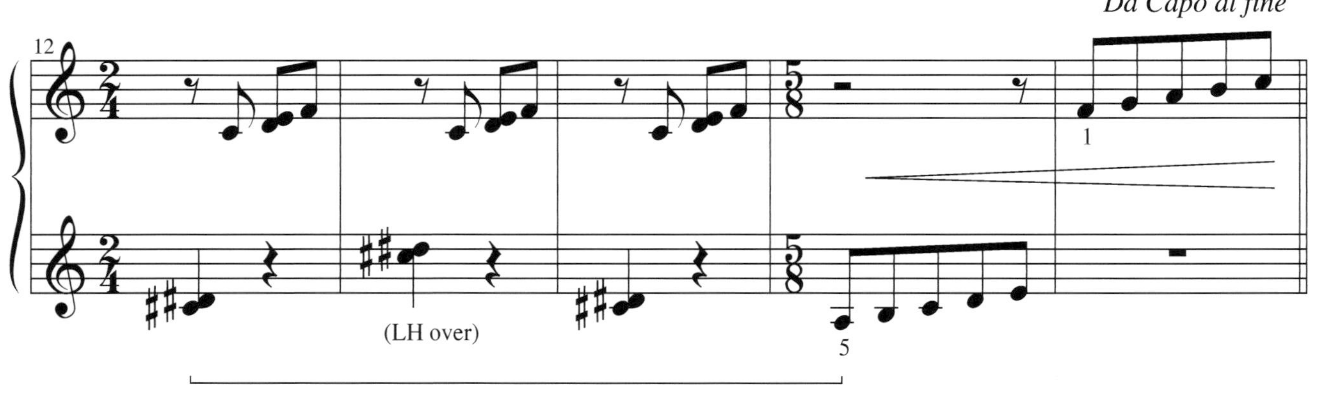

Folk Song

Béla Bartók, 1909

* Accidentals stay in effect for the entire measure.   From *For Children, Book II*, No. 10. The Fallen Soldier. Budapest, 1909

What Wondrous Love Is This?

German Dance

The Revenge of Debbie

13
f
16
5
2 4 5
decresc.
19
p
pp

The Entertainer

Scott Joplin
Arr. WDL

Capriccio

Allegro
Vincent Persichetti
mp
(2nd. time only)
(4)
mf
p
cresc.
f
ff

Root Position Triads

For Level One piano, you will be required to play root position major and minor triads on any note. Major triads are constructed from a Perfect 5th (P5) and a Major 3rd (M3); minor triads are constructed from a Perfect (P5) and a minor 3rd (m3):

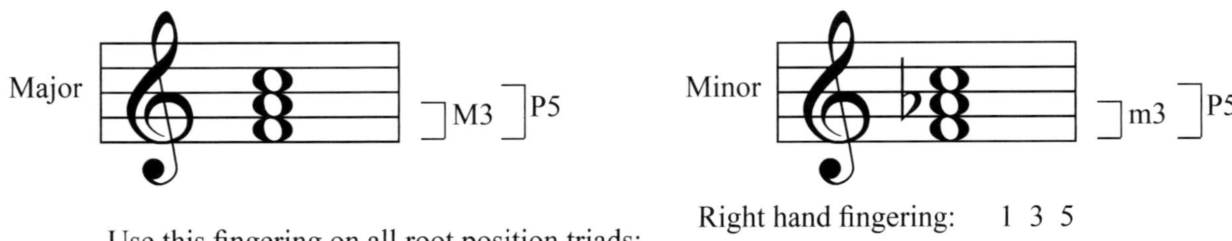

Here is the first set of triads (all the Major/minor triads on the white keys). If there is no accidental in front of a note then it should be considered a natural.

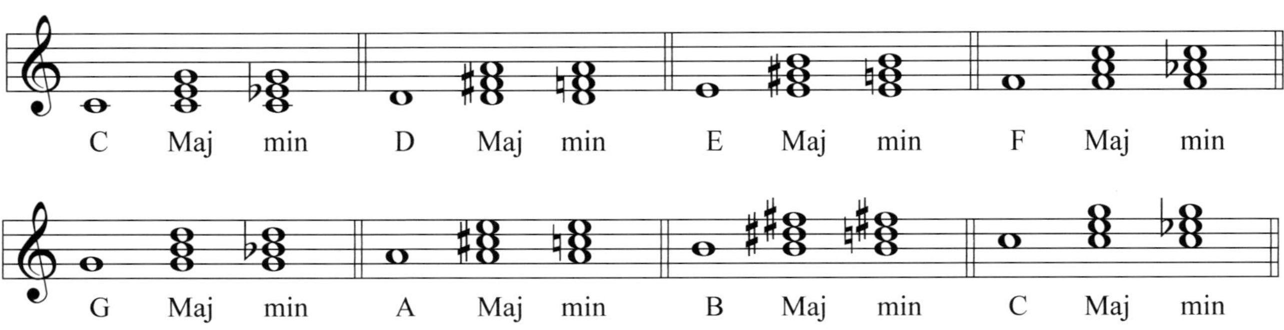

The next set of triads are all the Major/minor triads on the black notes. They are presented here in pairs, for example C#/Db; D#/Eb, etc. For the purposes of actually playing the triad, it doesn't matter which version you use. For example, if A# Major triad seems complicated to you, then use its ENHARMONIC spelling, Bb Major. If there is no accidental in front of a note then it should be considered a natural.

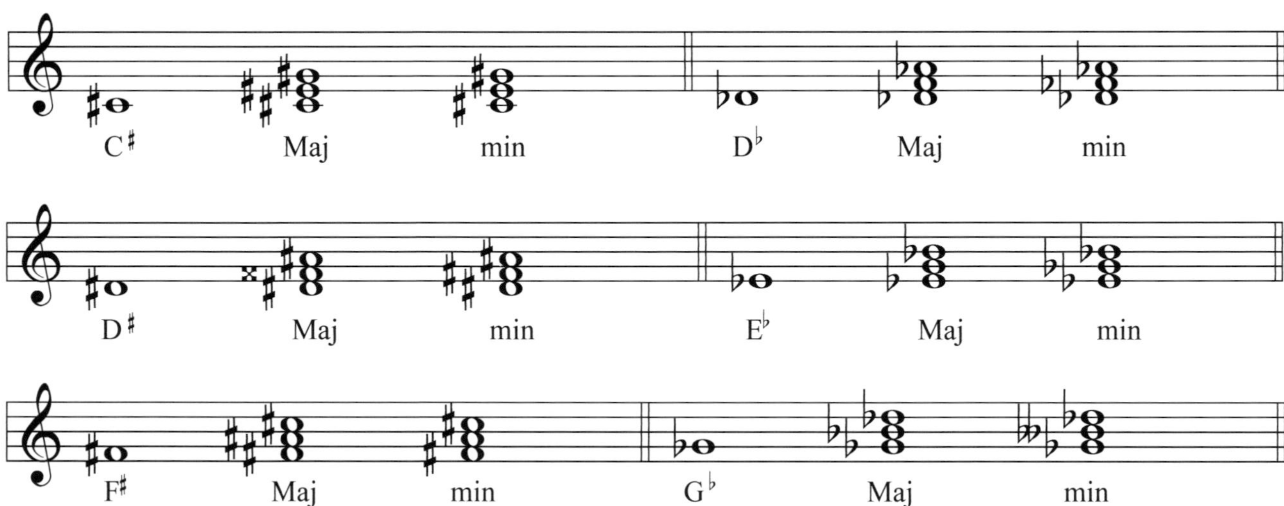

(Major/minor triads continued)

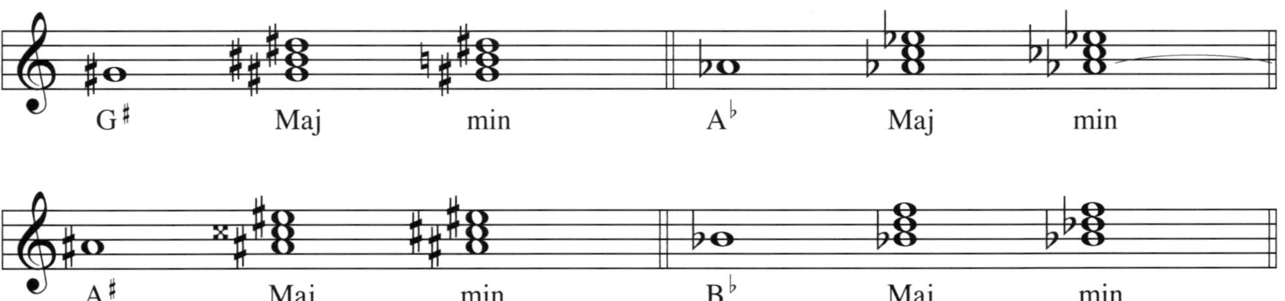

Here is a graphic representation of selected triads:

C Maj	C min	C# min
D Maj	D min	D# min
E Maj	E min	E♭ min
F Maj	F min	F# min
G Maj	G min	G# min
A Maj	A min	A# min
B Maj	B min	B♭ min

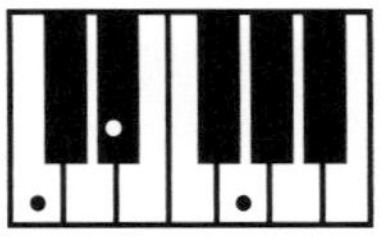

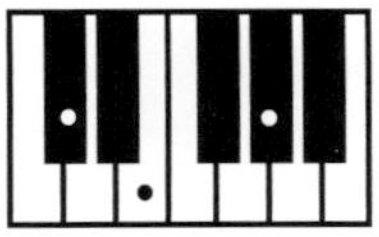

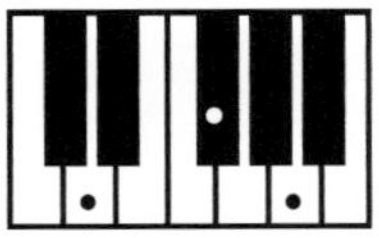

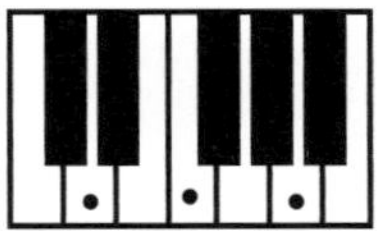

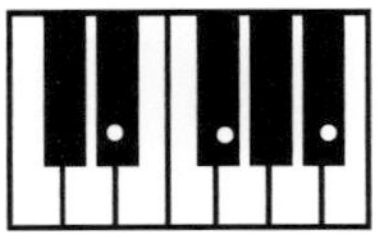

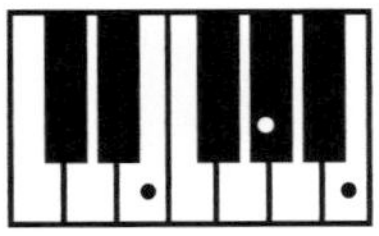

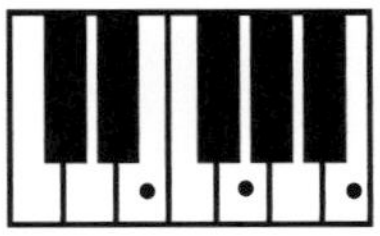

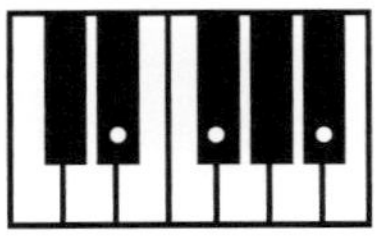

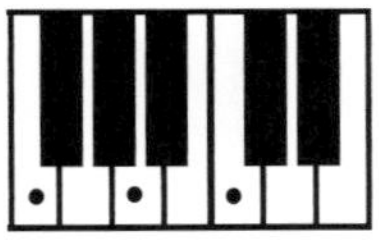

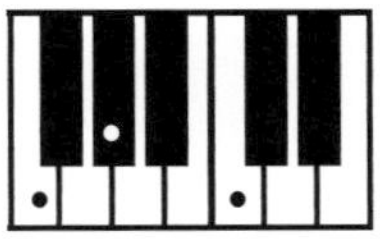

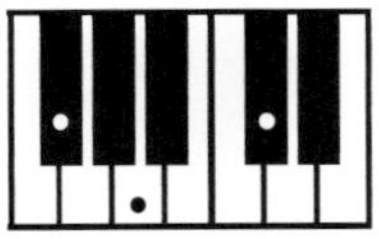

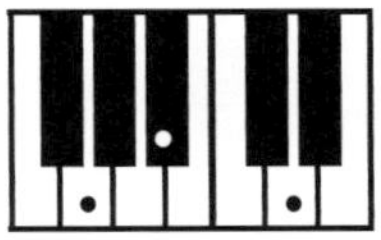

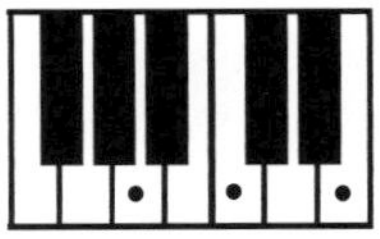

Block-Chord Cadences

"Block-chord" means all chords are   with 3 notes in each hand and each chord is identified by its Roman Numeral, not by its inversion. The following are "block-chord" style cadences. Here, "cadence" means a succession of chords (such as   I-IV-I-V7-I) and does not refer to what happens at the end of a phrase as described in Appendix II.

* The actual figured bass would be expressed: I   IV$^6_4$ I   V$^6_5$ I

Accompaniment Patterns

One way to harmonize a melody is to simply use the BLOCK-CHORDS from the cadences on page 34. However, a more interesting accompaniment can be accomplished by superimposing patterns on the block-chords as demonstrated below:

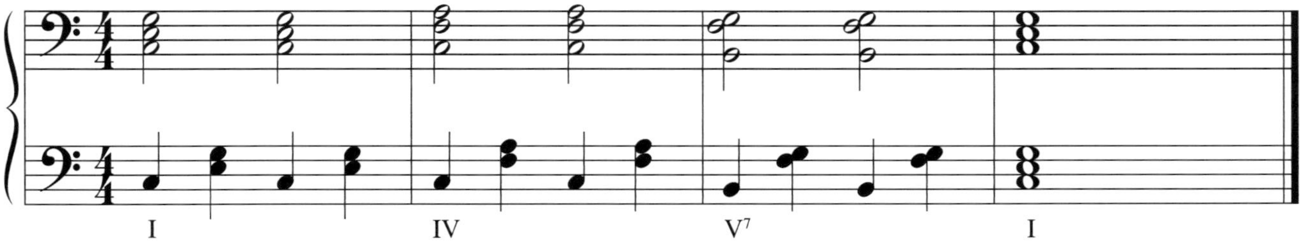

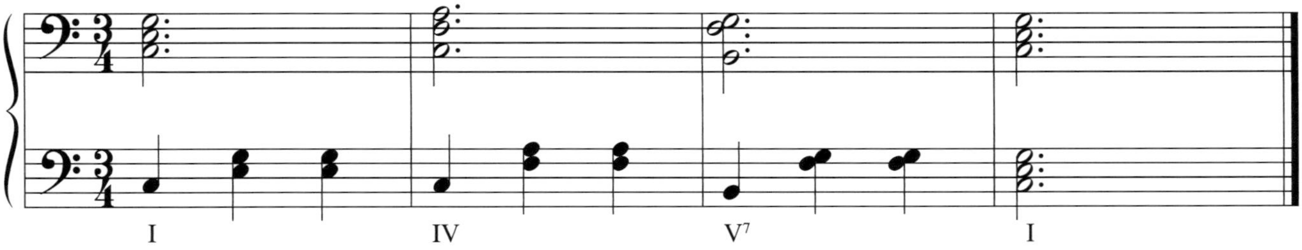

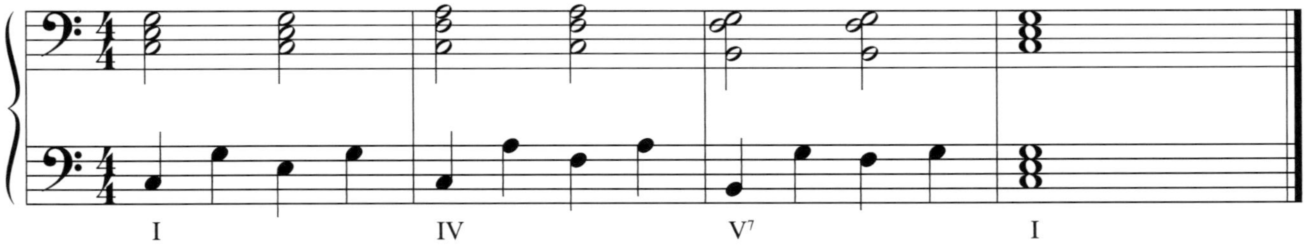

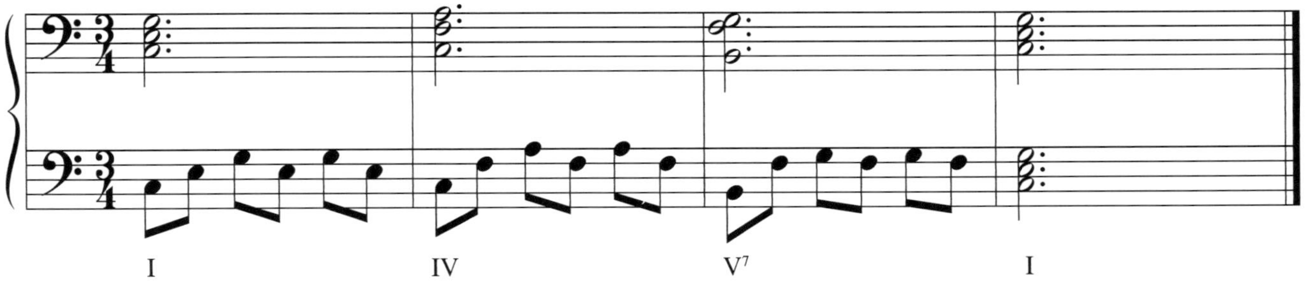

Here's an actual melody written out using Accompaniment Pattern #1

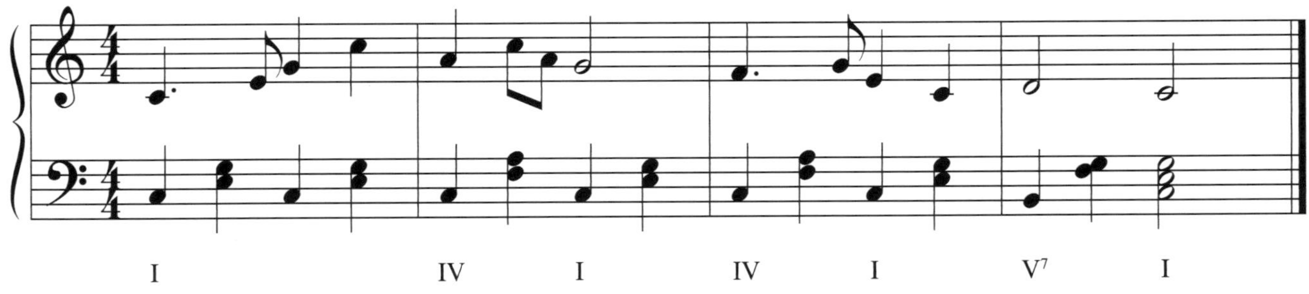

Procedures for Harmonizing Melodies

1. Memorize the appropriate cadence and be able to play it in the key of the melody.

2. For now, always harmonize the second degree of the scale (major or minor key) with a V7 chord.

3. In most cases, the 1st and last chord of the melody will alwasy be a I (i) chord.

4. If possible, avoid V^7 - IV. This is not ALWAYS possible, but generally try to avoid it.

5. Ask yourself these questions:

    a. Is the melody note I'm trying to harmonize in the chord I'm trying to use? If it isn't then it probably
    won't work. (See: **Appendix IV: Non-Chord Tones.**)

    b. Does the shape of the melody suggest a specific chord? If the melody outlines a specific triad or
    seventh chord then that is a good indication for the chord that should be used.

6. Write in the symbols for the chords you intend to play. For now, only use the chord voicings of the
    cadences you practiced.

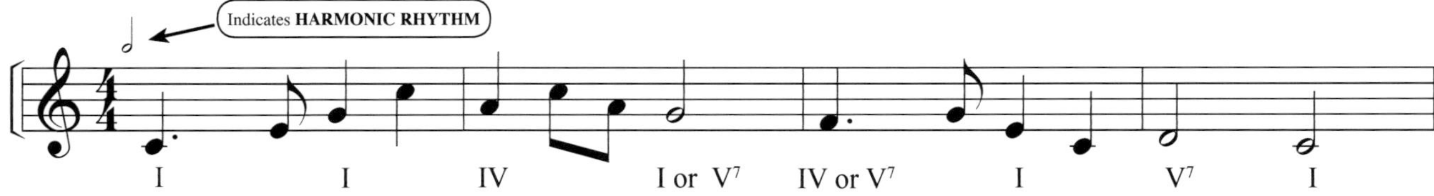

In the above melody segment, make the following observations:

- The HARMONIC RHYTHM is a half note (see below).

- The first measure outlines the I chord. Also, it's a good idea to always start with the I chord.

- The first two beats of the second measure outlines part of the IV chord.

- The "G" on beat three is not in the IV chord but IS in the I chord or the V^7 chord . If you use the I chord
  you can go to either I or V^7 for the next chord (beat 1, measure 3). However, if you use the V^7 chord,
  you HAVE to also use the V^7 chord for the 1st beat of measure 3 (see rule # 3 above). Probably it's best
  to use the I chord.

- The first two notes of measure three are both contained in the V^7 chord, so that is a logical choice.
  However, the "f" on beat one is also in the IV chord so that would work too. If you use the IV chord on
  beat 1 then the "G" on the "and" of beat 2 becomes an "escape" tone and THAT'S OK even though it's
  not in the IV chord. See: **Appendix IV: Non-Chord Tones.**

- The first beat of measure four is the second degree of the scale. Therefore, it is automatically harmonized by the V^7 chord (rule #2 above). The last note of measure four is in the I chord and it's generally a good idea to harmonize the final note of a melody with the I chord.

IN GENERAL:

- You may harmonize each melody note one at a time, or . . .
- You may harmonize the melody using a strict "harmonic rhythm." See the above example.

HARMONIC RHYTHM means:

"A rhythmically strict progression of chords." In the above example the harmonic rhythm is a half note (one chord every two beats). The harmonic rhythm may be anything that sounds good. However, the best harmonic rhythm depends upon such factors as tempo, style, etc. A typical harmonic rhythm would be either one or two chords per measure. Also, tempo affects decisions regarding the harmonic rhythm. Generally, if the tempo is fast then use a slower harmonic rhythm. If the tempo is slow then use a faster harmonic rhythm.

Here's a harmonized version of the melody on the previous page written out as you might play it using the simple cadence chord voicings:

Here's another version using the same chords but implementing one of the accompaniment patterns:

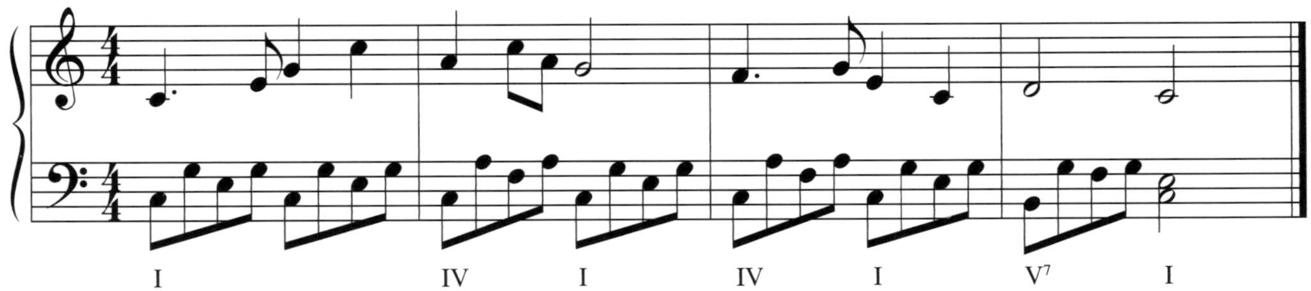

Try playing the above melody using one of the other accompaniment patterns.

For more DETAILED information regarding harmonizing melodies, please see Appendix 2: Melodic Phrases and Appendix 3: Melodic Cadences.

Melodies for Harmonization

WDL
6
Harmonize each melody note.
HAMBURG
Lowell Mason, 1824
7
V7
WDL
8
LIGHTLY ROW
Folk Song
9
Harmonize each melody note - slow tempo
LOW DUTCH
Bay Psalm Book, 1698 edition
10

Folk Song
11
WDL
12
NINETY-FIFTH
Wyeth's, Repository of Sacred Music, Part 2nd, 1820
13
Folk Song
14
Be Creative.
WDL
15

MELODY
Robert Schumann
16
FOUNDATION
Union Harmony, 1837
17
WALTZ
Franz Schubert
18
Folk Song
19

42

MINUET
J. S. Bach
HOLY MANA
Kentucky Harmony, 1825
FOLK SONG
Harmonize beats 1 and 3
AMAZING GRACE
Virginia Harmony, 1831
20
21
22
23

DARK EYES
Hungarian Folk Song
24
SHE'LL BE COMIN' ROUND THE MOUNTAIN
American Folk Song
25
WALTZ
Folk Song
26
REAPER'S SONG
Robert Schumann
27
= 1st time. 2nd time harmonize each melody note.
BLUE SKY
American Folk Song
28

Improvisation

The goal for improvisation skills in Secondary Piano is to improvise simple melodies over a given chord progression. In Level One the improvisation examples will consist of:

1. Primary chords in major and minor keys through two accidentals.
2. Improvised melodies should consist of chord tones.
3. The range of the improvisation should be about a 4th (for example, use scale degrees 1 - 4).
4. Improvised melodies should generally make use of a RHYTHMIC MOTIVE.
5. Use a consistent HARMONIC RHYTHM (for example, 1 or 2 chords per measure).

Improvisation involves spontaneously making up a melody over a given chord progression. The chord voicings required in Level 2 piano will be the same as those found in the bock-chord cadences earlier in this book. If you need to review the differences between chord tones and non-chord tones, see **Appendix IV** for a detailed explanation. All the improvisation examples in Level 2 piano will involve improvising melodies consisting of a combination of chord tones and non-chord tones. Here is a written-out example demonstrating basic requirements for this level:

Consider the following example:

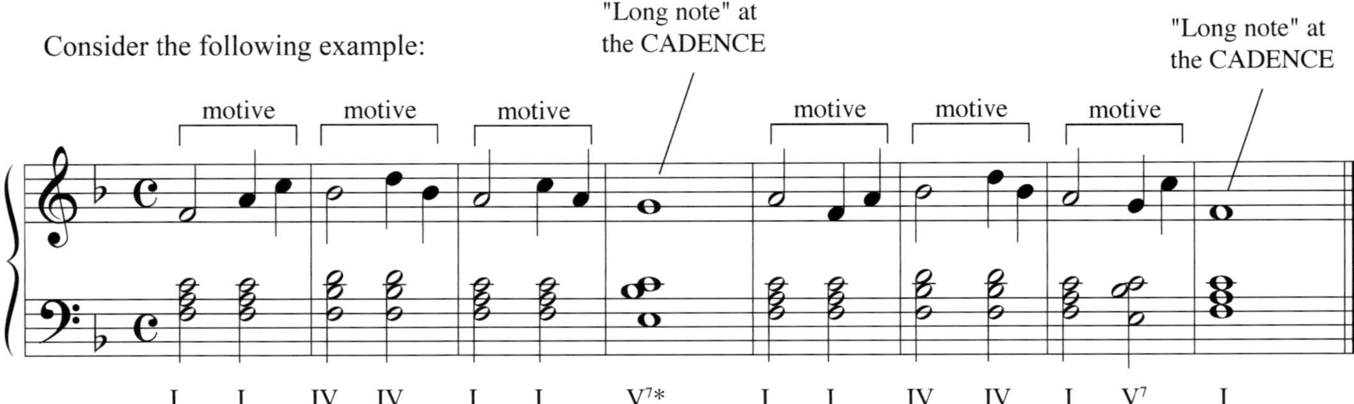

In the above example all melody notes are contained in the chords which harmonize them (they are "chord-tones"). The "G's" in measure 4 and measure 7 may seem to be non-chord tones because they do not appear in the accompanying chord. However, actually they do. The V^7 chord in the key of F major is spelled C-E-G-Bb. Sometimes the 5th of a 7th chord is omitted and that is the case for the V^7 voicing used in all the block-chord cadences.

Notice how the rhythm for the melody is the same in each measure except for the whole notes in measures 4 and 8. This repetitive rhythm is called a "rhythm motive." In music, a MOTIVE is a short melodic and/or rhythmic idea used as a constructional element. In other words, a MOTIVIC IDEA is used over and over again to build up a larger section or an entire composition. [Consider a brick wall. A single brick is a "motive" and the wall is constructed by using the "brick motive" over and over again until an entire wall is built.]

The short example above is a complete melody which consists of TWO musical PHRASES. The PHRASES are set apart by the whole notes in measures 4 and 8 and these POINTS OF REST within the melody are called CADENCES. It is often easy to find the CADENCE POINTS in any melody -- just look for the longest note values, particularly if they occur in groups of 4 or 8 measures. FOUR-MEASURE PHRASES are common in all styles of Western music and often the cadence point will have the LONGEST NOTE of the phrase. [For more on PHRASES and CADENCES, see: APPENDIX 2: MELODIC PHRASES and Appendix 3: Cadences.] You can make your improvised melodies sound like REAL MELODIES if you structure them like REAL MELODIES:

1. Use a simple rhythmic motive.
2. Use LONG NOTES (whole notes, dotted half notes, etc.) at the cadence points (meas. 4 and 8).
3. Always end with the tonic note (1st degree of the scale). The majority of successful melodies in Western music end on the tonic note. "Successful melodies" are those melodies which have been IN USE for a long period of time, for example, 50 years, 100 years, etc. Look through the melodies in the Harmonized Melodies section of this book and you will discover that they ALL end on the tonic note.

The goal for Level One piano is to be able to improvise chord tones over a given chord progression. Try improvising a melody consisting only of chord tone in the following example. The first measure has been done for you and you should use this MOTIVE in each measure throughout the example except at the cadence points where you see the whole notes.

Improvise a melody for the following example using the rhythmic motive in first measure. Repeat in the keys of C and F. Use long notes (whole notes) at the cadence points.

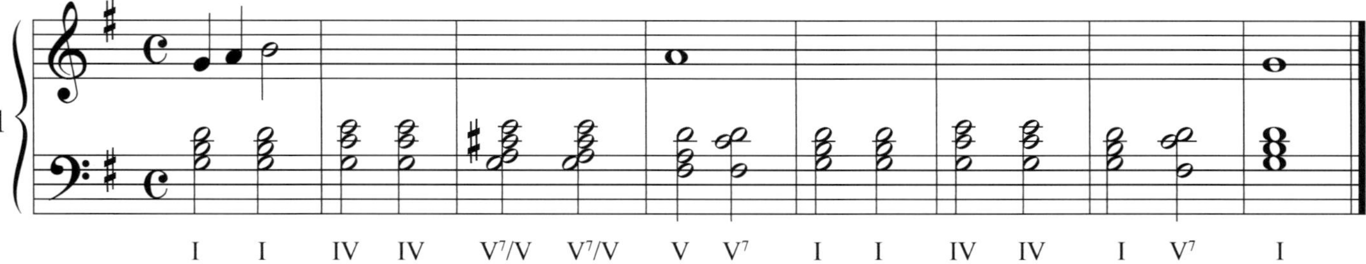

Do:

1. Use chord tones, passing tones, and neighbor tones. If you need to, consult the example on the previous page.
2. Generally, keep the overall range of your improvisation within about a 5th or 6th. You may want to start out with a limited range of a 3rd and then gradually increase the range to 5th or 6th.
3. If you have trouble with the coordination aspect, try "patting" the rhythm of the right hand while you play the chords in the left hand. It's always a good idea to practice counting outloud while you play.
4. Try starting your improvisation on a scale degree other than the 1st scale degree (for example the 3rd of the 5th).

Don't:

1. Don't write out your improvisation. Make it up (improvise it) every time.

When you feel comfortable playing the example above in the written key of F major, try playing it in the keys of C major and G major.

Improvise a melody for the following example using the rhythmic motive in first measure. Repeat in the keys of C and G. Use long notes (whole notes) at the cadence points.

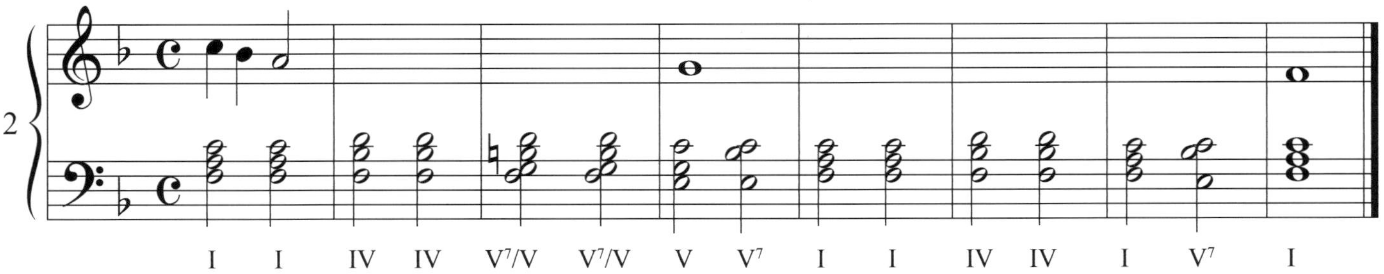

Improvisation, Part II: More on Rhythmic Motives

As described earlier, a MOTIVE is a short melodic and/or rhythmic idea used as a constructional element. Many successful melodies use non-motivic melodic construction. However, the efforts of novice improvisers to play non-motivic improvisations often sound "rambling" -- that is, the improvised melody rambles in an almost random way, not having any real sense of direction, strong cadence points, or any sense of tension/relaxation or climax. A melody or improvisation will have a greater sense of unity and direction (including climax and cadence) if it is constructed motivically, especially for someone just learning to improvise.

To begin to develop a good concept of rhythmic motive, write out four (4) one-measure rhythmic motives for each of the meters below. Individual melody notes are inconsequential at this point. The actual melody notes will later be determined by the given chords. For now, use any pitches you want or just use one pitch. To be a VIABLE rhythmic motive, your rhythmic motive must have at least TWO different rhythmic values, for example a half note and 2 quarter notes. Consequently, 4 quarter notes, 2 half notes, 8 eighth notes, etc. would not be viable rhythmic motives. Your rhythmic motives will be ONE measure long and will be the equivalent of 2 chords in length. For example, in 4/4/ time each chord would get 2 beats and there would be 2 chords in each measure; in 6/4 time each chord would get 3 beats and there would be 2 chords in each measure.

After you have completed the composition of your rhythmic motives, improvise complete melodies over the example chord progressions below by making use of one of your motives. Use ONE motive for the entire improvisation. Use a LONG note (dotted whole note) at the cadence points. Before you begin, analyze the chords and write them in the music below the chords. <u>DO NOT</u> WRITE OUT YOUR IMPROVISATION IN THE MUSIC, but you may sketch out your chosen rhythmic motive in the provided treble clef.

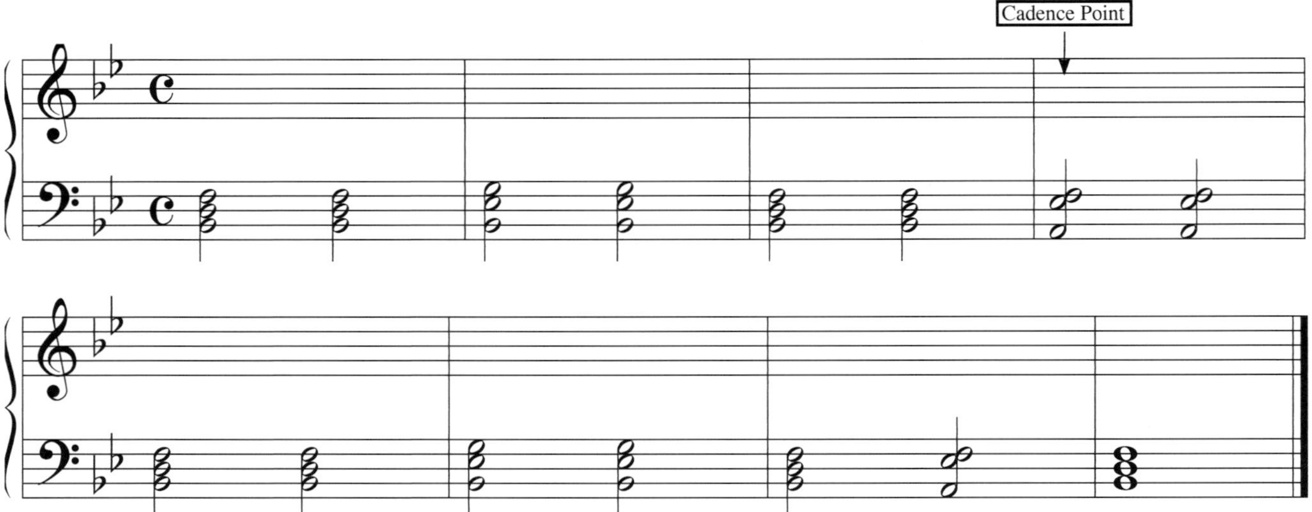

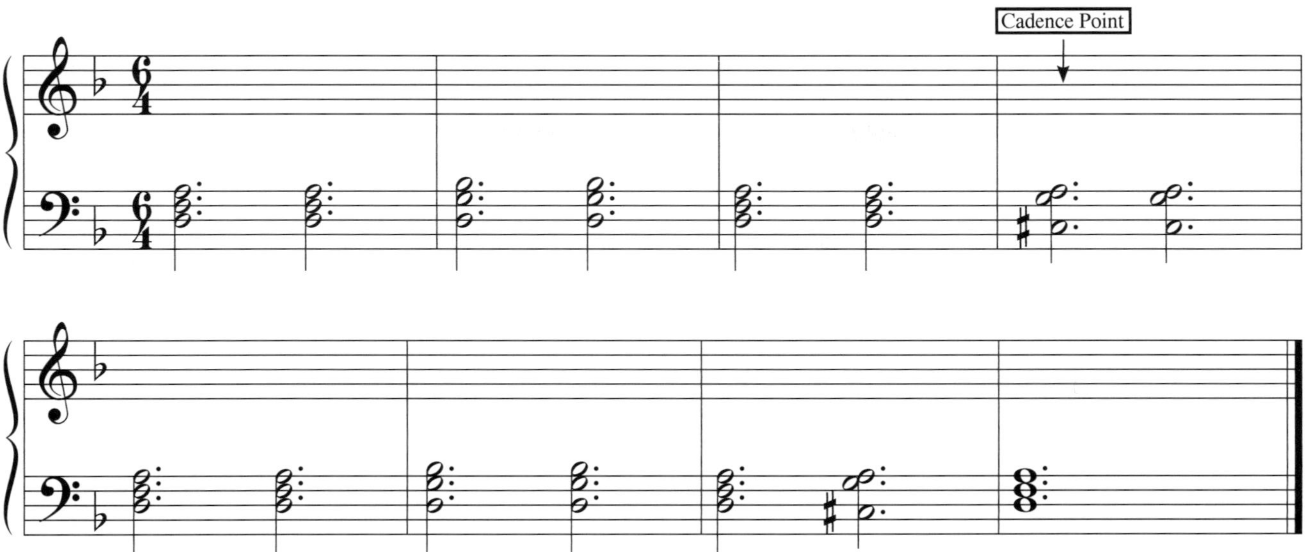

Improvisation: Improvised Melodies Over Chord Symbols

When you improvise melodies over chord progressions the voicings of the chords you play in the left hand should be the same as the cadence chords you have already learned. However, if your instructor agrees you may use any voicings you wish as long as you keep the rhythm correct and the tempo steady.

Practice the examples in the required keys for your cadences (through 2 accidentals. Each example is two phrases (2 lines) long. The next-to-last chord in each phrase is the "CADENCE POINT." Please follow these rules:

1. Play the cadence for the key in which you plan to improvise.
2. Play through the chord progression with just the left hand using the cadence voicings.
3. Use one of the rhythmic motives you wrote out on the previous page.
4. Play the chord progression with your left hand while you PAT the rhythmic motive with your right.
5. Play LONG notes (one note that lasts for 2 chords) at all the CADENCE POINTS.
6. Keep the range of your improvisation within a 5th or 6th (although you might start off with a range of a 3rd or 4th).
7. Create your improvisation using chord tones, passing tones and neighbor tones.
8. Generally, it is better to use more steps than skips.
9, Always end the improvisation on the tonic note.

#1	I	I	IV	IV	I	IV	V⁷	V⁷
	I	I	IV	IV	I	V⁷	I	I

#2	i	i	iv	iv	i	iv	V⁷	V⁷
	i	i	iv	iv	i	V⁷	i	i

#3	I	V⁷	I	I	IV	IV	V⁷	V⁷
	I	IV	I	I	IV	V⁷	I	I

#4	i	V⁷	i	i	iv	iv	V⁷	V⁷
	i	iv	i	i	iv	V⁷	i	i

For all these chord progressions:

1. Prepare each one TWICE: once with 2 beats for each chord and once with 3 beats for each chord.

2. Use one of the rhythmic motives you composed on the previous page.

3. The CADENCE POINT for each phrase is the next-to-last chord in each line. So, play a LONG note on that chord and don't continue your rhythmic motive. See the example at the beginning of this section as a model.

4. It's always a good idea to practice playing the chords with the left hand while you PAT your rhythmic motive with the right hand.

48

Improvisation, Part III: Improvised Melodies Over Chord Symbols
Primary Chords

Improvise melodies over the following chord progressions using techniques you have learned so far. The voicings you should use for the chords are the same voicings you have learned for the cadences earlier in this book. However, if your instructor agrees you may use any voicing you wish as long as you keep the rhythm correct and the tempo steady. For example, give each chord the correct number of beats.

Play each example in the following keys:

      Major: C D F G B$\flat$
      Minor: am bm dm em gm

Each example is two phrases (2 lines) long. You should prepare each improvisation twice: once giving each chord 2 beats, and once giving each chord 3 beats.

Please follow these procedures:

1. Play the cadence for the key in which you plan to improvise.
2. Play through the chord progression with just the left hand using the cadence voicings.
3. Use one of the rhythmic motives you wrote out earlier in this section.
4. Play the chord progression with your left hand while you PAT the rhythmic motive with your right.
5. Play LONG notes (one note that lasts for 2 chords) at all the CADENCE POINTS.
6. Keep the range of your improvisation within a 4th, although you might start off with only 2 notes
    (1st and 2nd scale degrees) and gradually work up to a range of a 4th.
7. Create your improvisation using chord tones only. Non-chord tones will be covered in later books.
8. Generally, it is better to use more steps than skips.
9, Always end the improvisation on the tonic note

Cadence Point

#								
1	I	I	IV	IV	I	I	V^7	V^7
	I	I	IV	IV	I	V^7	I	I
2	i	i	iv	iv	i	i	V^7	V^7
	i	i	iv	iv	i	V^7	i	i
3	I	IV	I	I	IV	IV	V^7	V^7
	I	IV	I	I	IV	V^7	I	I
4	i	iv	i	i	iv	iv	V^7	V^7
	i	iv	i	i	iv	V^7	i	i
5	I	V^7	I	I	IV	IV	V^7	V^7
	I	V^7	I	I	IV	V^7	I	I

Class Notes

Sight Reading and Transposition I: Piano Scores

WDL
WDL
WDL
WDL
5
6
7
8

WDL
9
WDL
10
WDL
11

WDL
JINGLE BELLS
Carol
MERRILY WE ROLL ALONG
American Folk Song

WDL
15
MY LORD, WHAT A MORNING
arr. by WDL
16
ST. FLAVIAN
17

SONATINA
WDL
18
LIGHTLY ROW
arr. by WDL
19

Sight Reading and Transposition II: Open Scores

Antonio Vivaldi
from *Gloria*

Anonymous
c. 1600

Jacob Arcadelt
Ave Maria

3

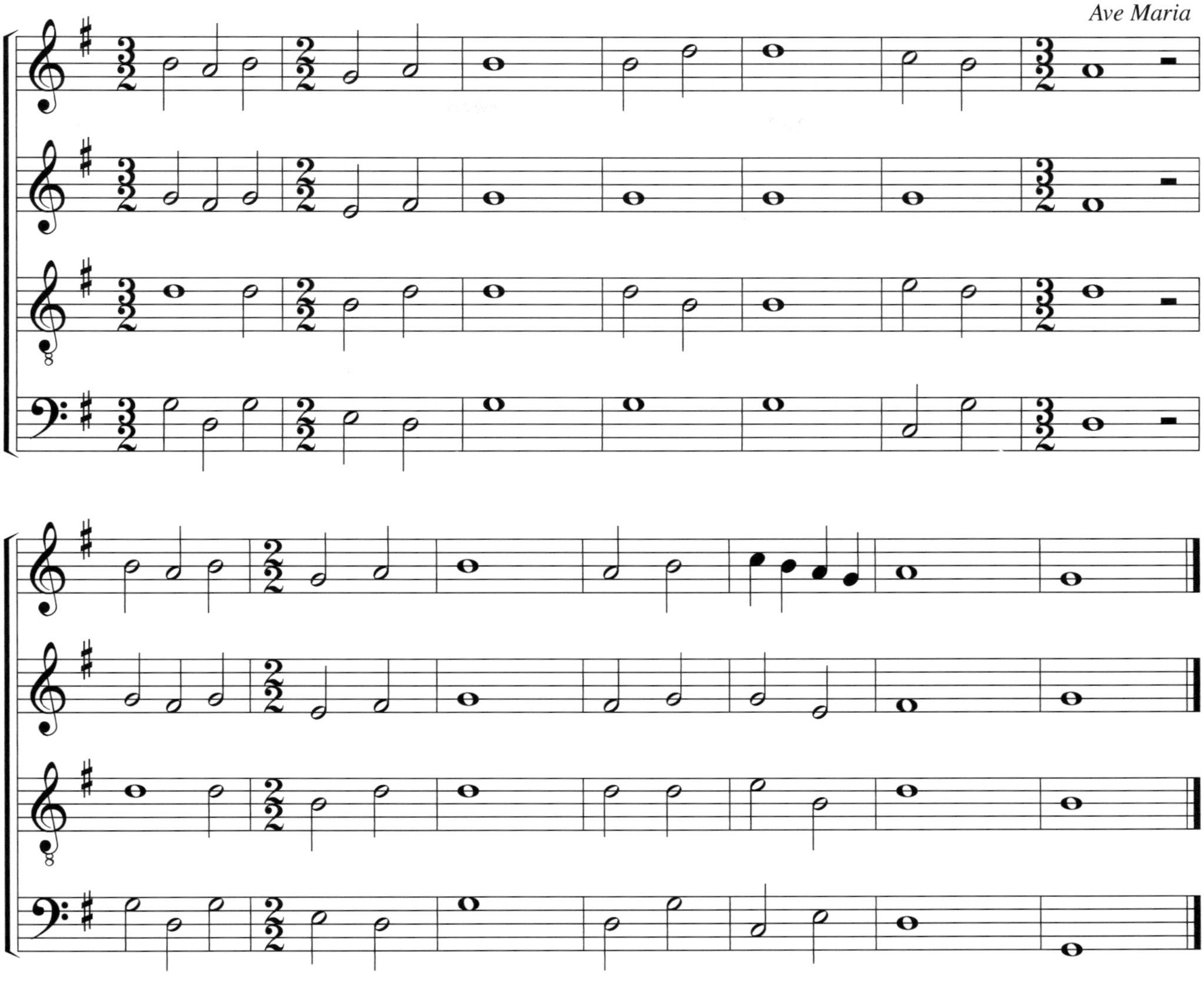

IN BABILONE
Traditional Dutch Melody

4

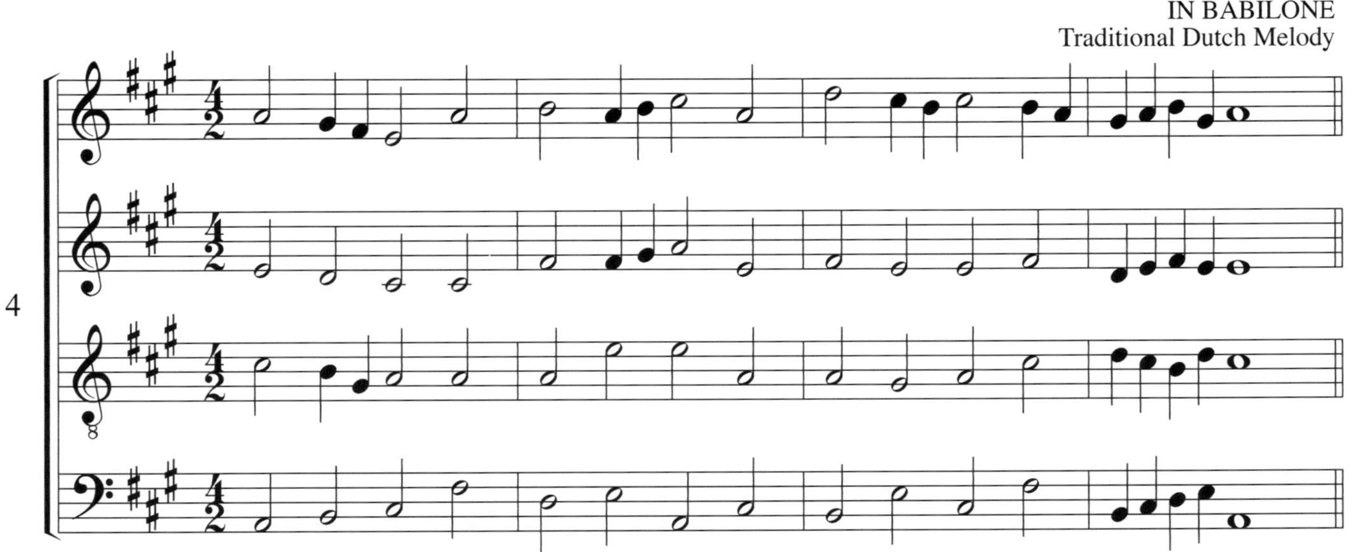

G.F. Handel

W.A. Mozart
from *Cosi fan Tutti*

Wm. Brade
Canzon, c. 1600

7

Saint-Saëns
from *Christmas Oratorioz*

8

Bernardo Pisano
Trio, c. 1520
9
7

Michael Praetorius
Lo, How a Rose e'er Blooming
10

Score reading #11

Igor Stravinsky
from *l'Oiseau de Feu*, 1910

(Score reading #11, cont'd)
63
Molto pesante
Fl. 1
Fl. 2
Ob.
Cl.
Bsns.
F. Hns.
Tpts.
Trb. 1
Trbs. 2&3
Tuba
Timp.
Perc. 1
Triangle
Perc. 2
Piatti
Gr.C.
Vln. 1
Vln. 2
Viola
Cello
Bass
sempre più cresc.
sempre più cresc.
pp subito
ffff
sffz

Scales

All major and minor scales can be divided into 3 "groups" according to their fingering patterns. Each group has its own characteristics and these are listed below. It is recommended that the student memorize each group of scales along with their characteristics and fingerings. Here are some general, introductory statements about scale fingerings.

1. In any scale (major or minor), the 4th finger in each hand only plays ONCE per octave. Consequently, the 4th finger always plays the SAME note. One way to think about scale fingerings is simply to know (memorize) the 4th finger note of each scale.

2. Fingering in scales is CONSECUTIVE, that is -- don't skip fingers. This is a common mistake, particularly skipping the 2nd finger.

Group I Scales: Those scales in which the thumbs always play together.

MAJOR KEYS (thumb notes)		**MINOR KEYS** (thumb notes)	
D-Flat	F & C	b-flat	c & f
G-Flat	C-flat & F	e-flat	f & c-flat
B	B & E	b	b & e
F	F & C	f	f & c

Here are some characteristics which may help to play these scales using the correct fingering:

1. The thumbs of each hand always play together. In addition, each scale in this group has 2 thumb notes (see the above chart). The thumbs always play on the white notes — never on black notes.

2. For all the scales in this group, the 2nd and 3rd fingers of each hand play on or near the group of 2 black notes. The 2nd, 3rd, & 4th fingers of each hand play on or near the group of 3 black notes.

Group I Scales

All scales should be played from memory, 2 octaves ascending and descending in a steady tempo with correct fingering.

Group I Scales, cont'd

Group I Scales, cont'd

Group I Arpeggios

All arpeggios should be played from memory, 2 octaves ascending and descending in a steady tempo with correct fingering. Unlike scales, there are several sets of fingering which different teachers use to teach arpeggios. You should use the fingering your instructor recommends. However, below is outlined a commonly used set of arpeggio fingering.

As with scales, arpeggios can be grouped according to specific fingering patterns. However, the groups of scales and arpeggios are not the same event thought there are coincidently three groups of arpeggio fingering.

GROUP I (fingered like C Major):   Right hand: 1 2 3 1 2 3 5
                                           Left hand: 5 4 2 1 4 2 1

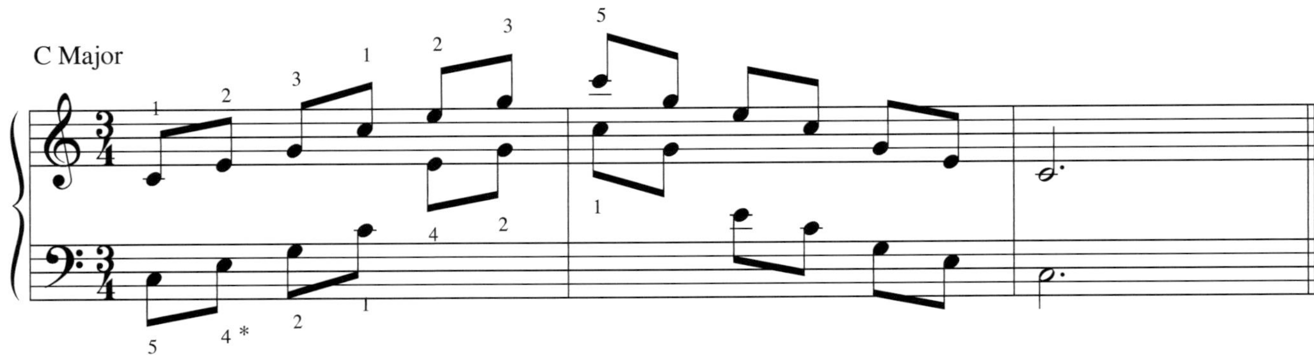

* Be sure to use the 4th finger in the left hand.

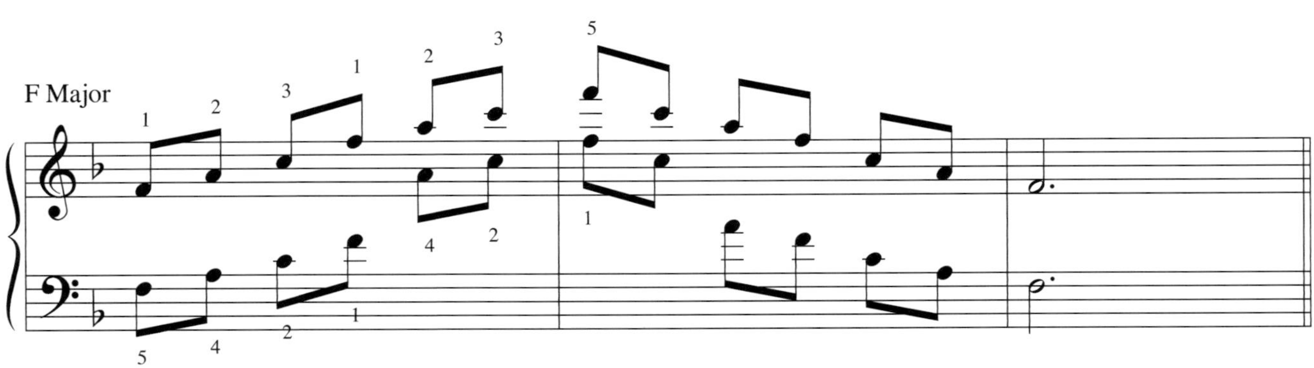

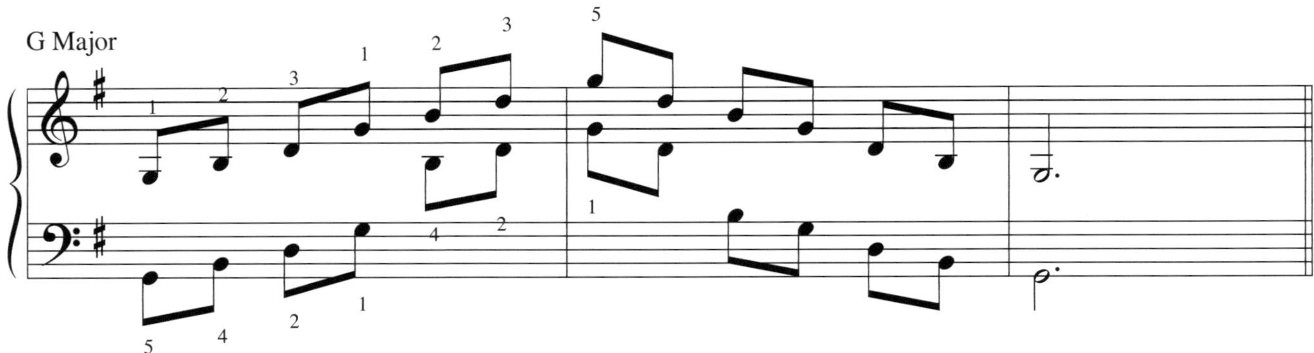

Group I Arpeggios, cont'd

Group I Arpeggios, cont'd

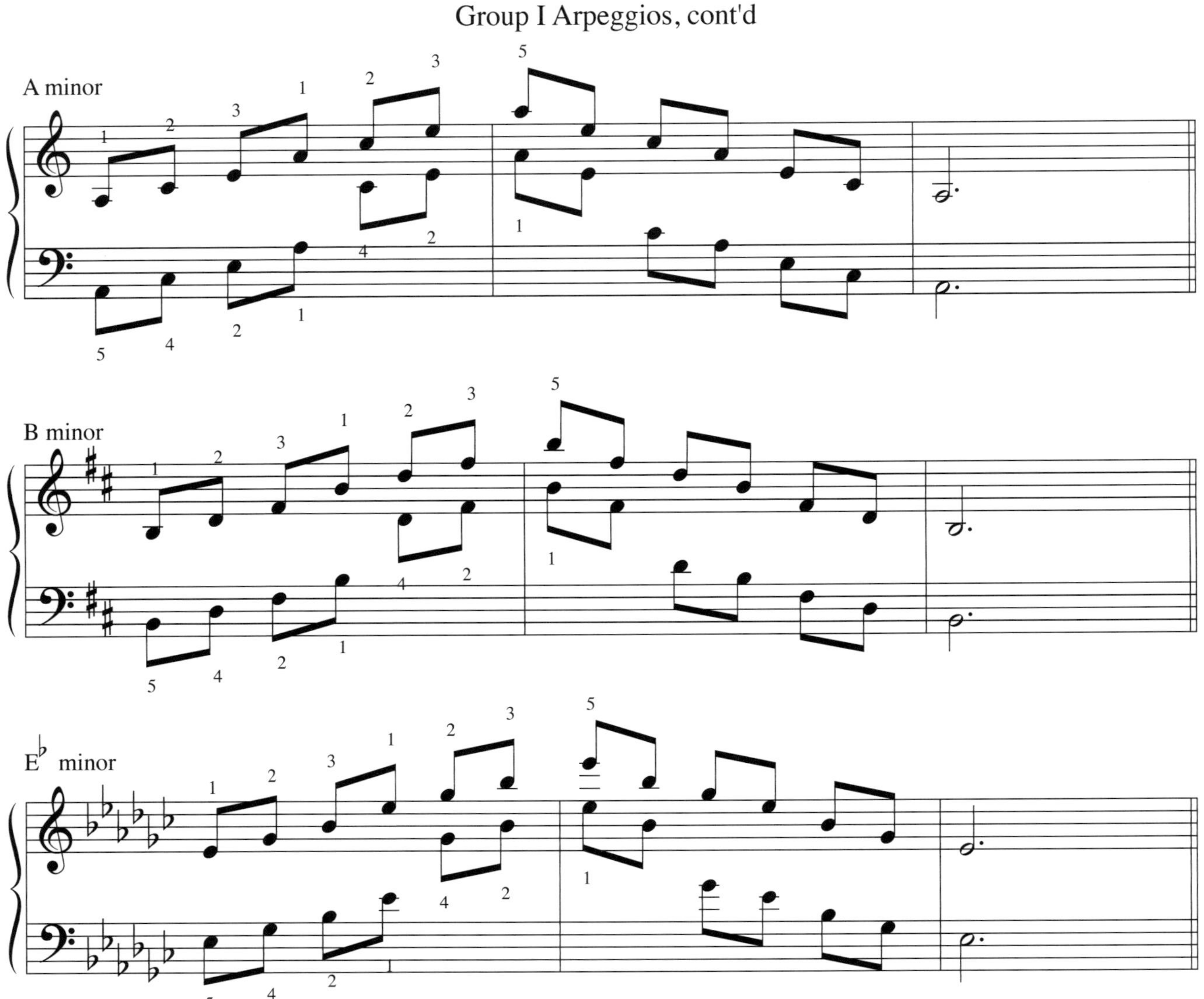

Scale and Arpeggio Practice Log

Scales	1	2	3	4	5	6	7	8	9	10	11	12	13	14	15	16	17	18	19
D-flat																			
G-flat																			
B																			
F																			
B-flat minor																			
E-flat minor																			
B minor																			
F minor																			

Arpeggios	1	2	3	4	5	6	7	8	9	10	11	12	13	14	15	16	17	18	19
C																			
F																			
G																			
C minor																			
D minor																			
E minor																			
F minor																			
G minor																			
A minor																			
B minor																			
E-flat minor																			

Exercises

Exercise #1 Ascending

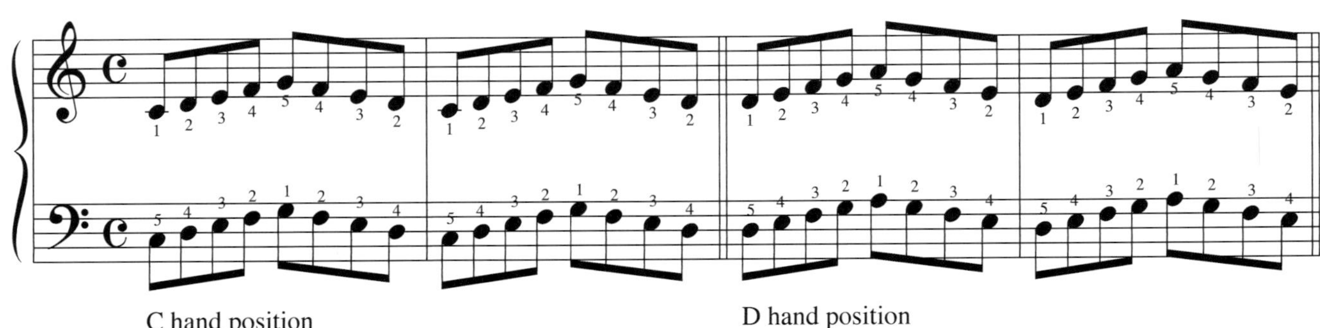

C hand position   D hand position

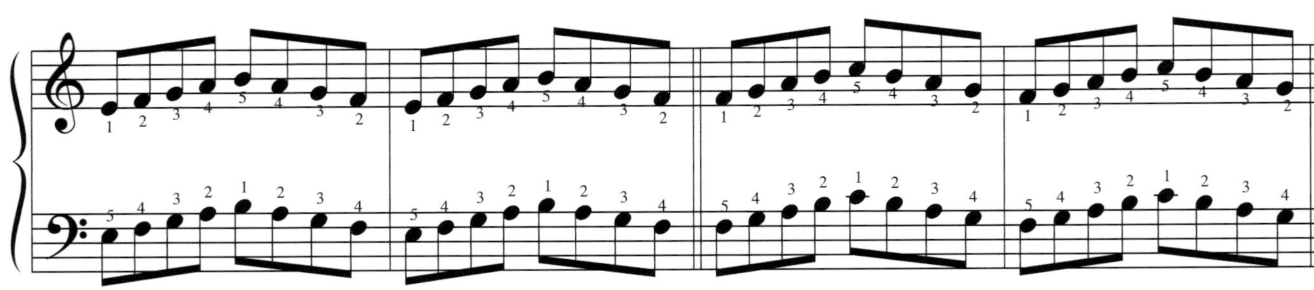

E hand position   F hand position

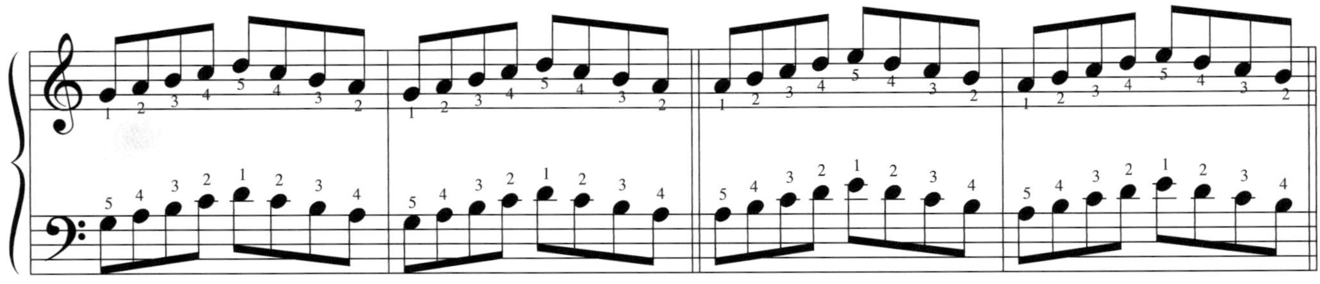

G hand position   A hand position

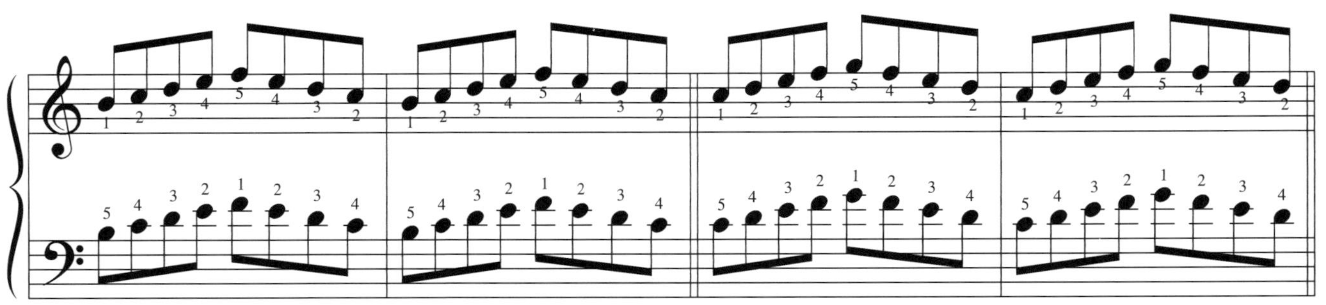

B hand position   C hand position

Exercise #1 Descending

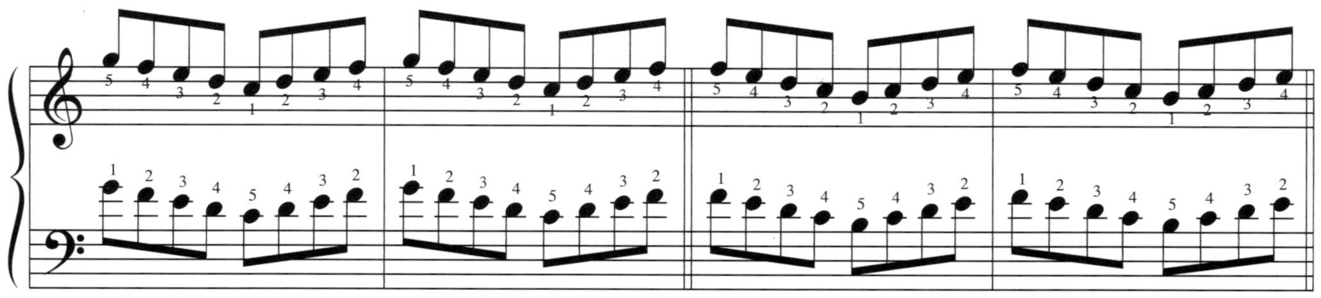

C hand position   B hand position

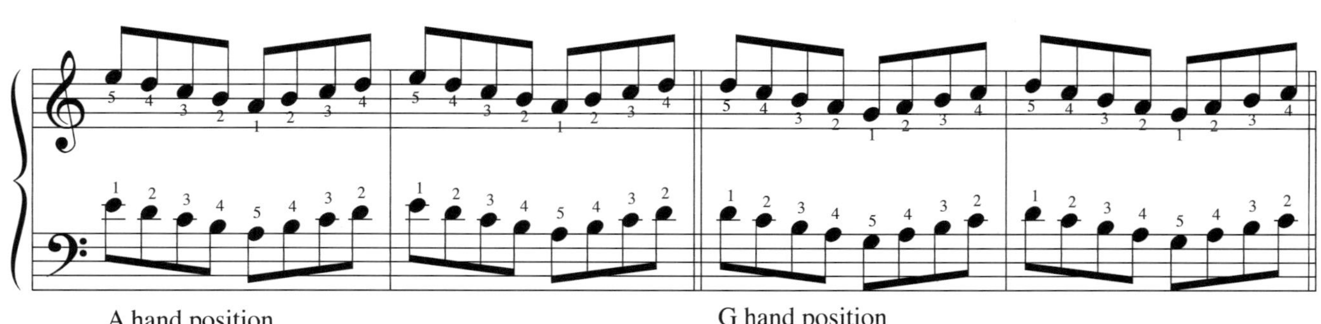

A hand position   G hand position

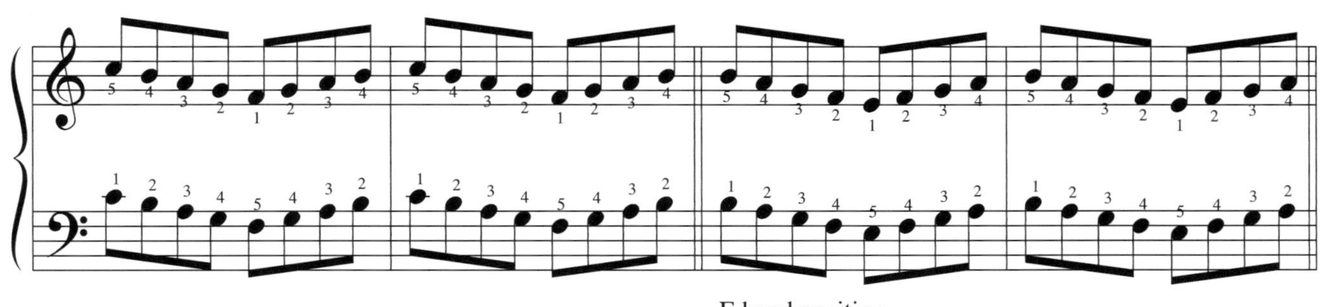

F hand position   E hand position

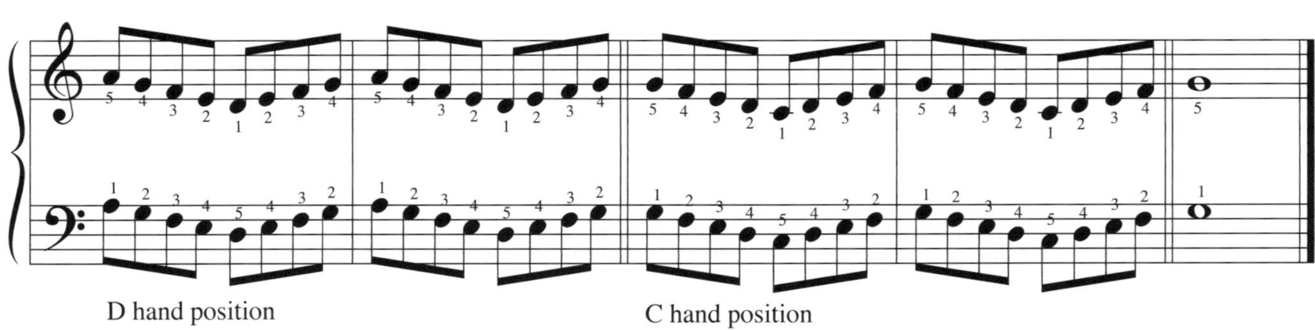

D hand position   C hand position

Exercise #2 Ascending

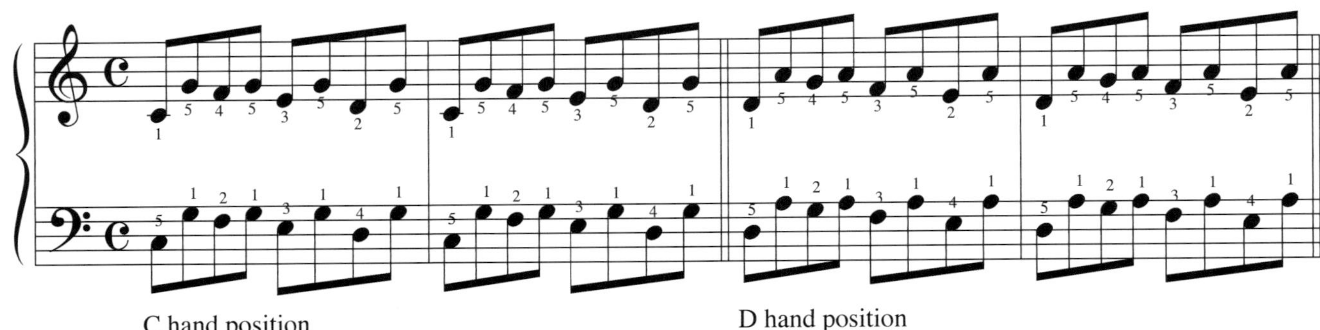

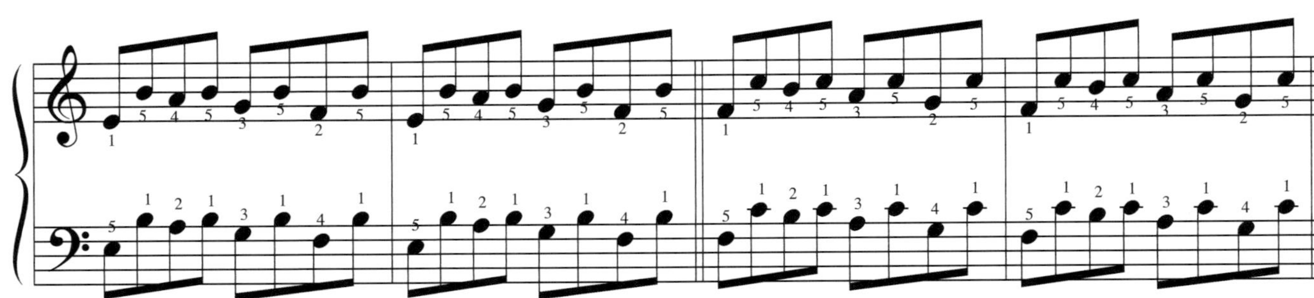

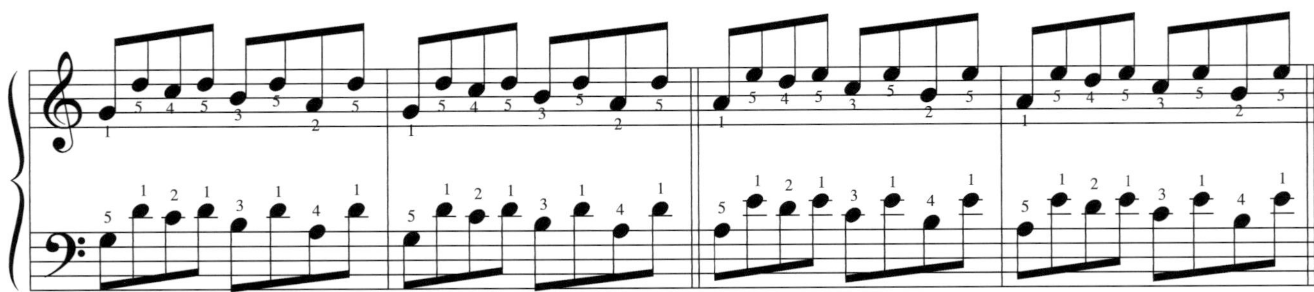

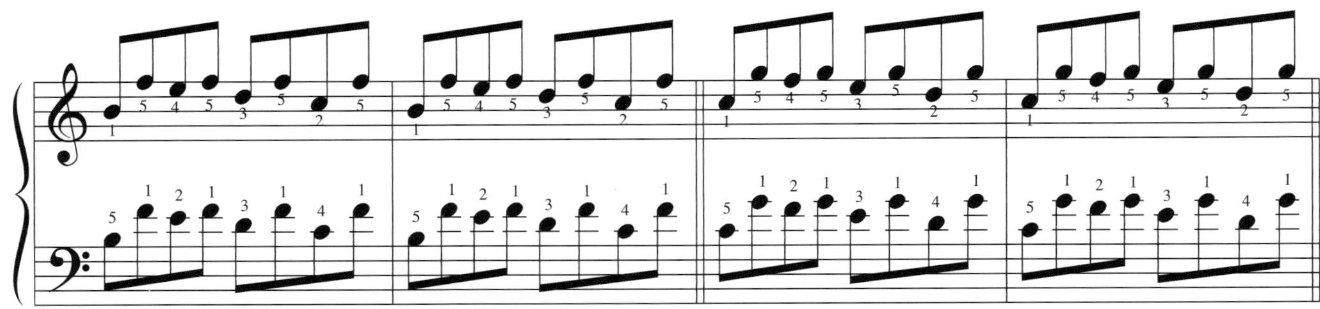

Exercise #2 Descending

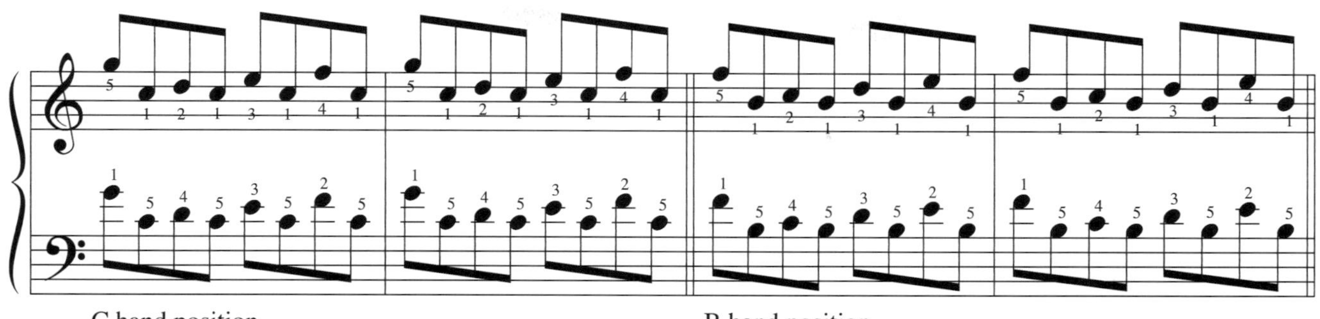

C hand position   B hand position

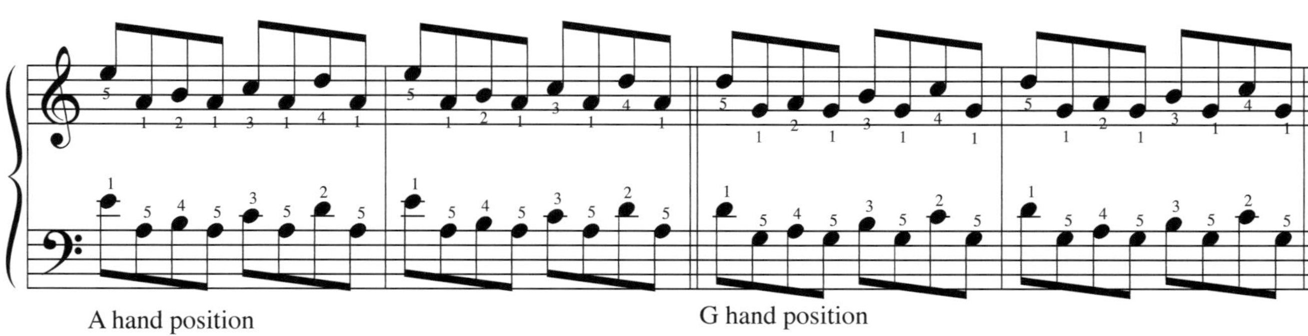

A hand position   G hand position

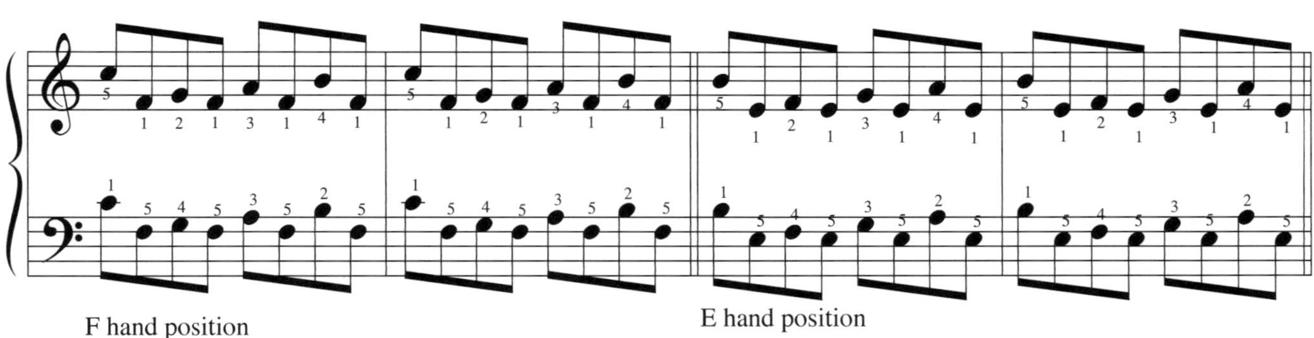

F hand position   E hand position

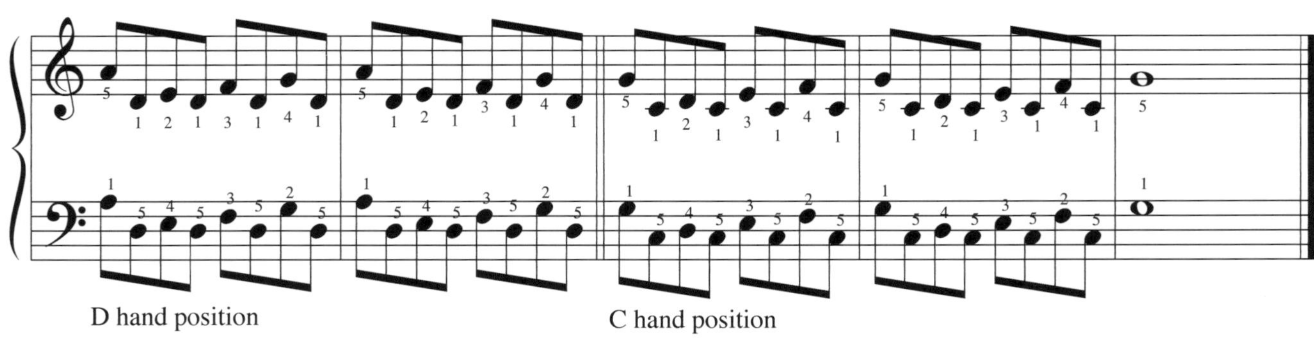

D hand position   C hand position

Exercise #3 Ascending

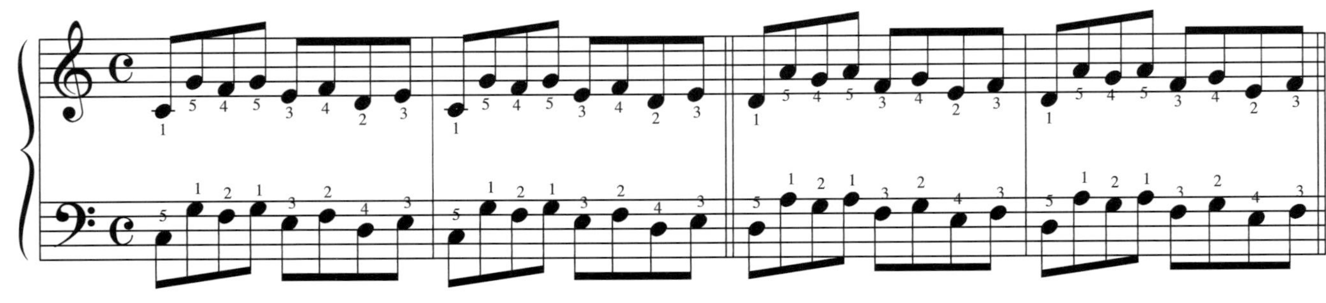

C hand position   D hand position

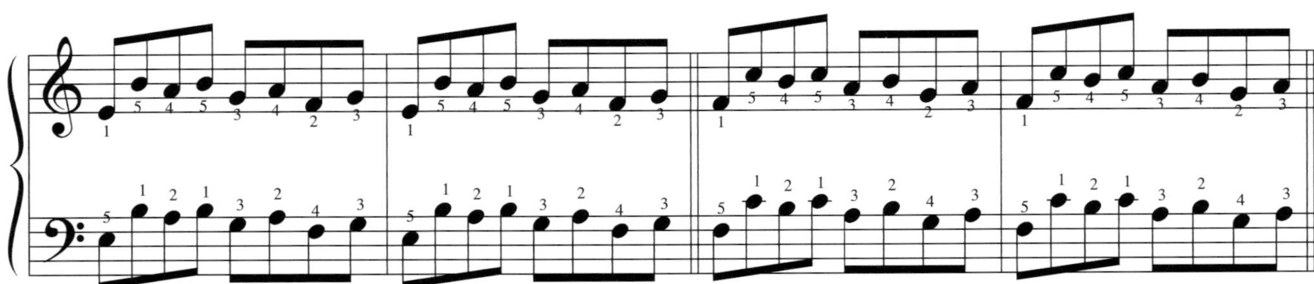

E hand position   F hand position

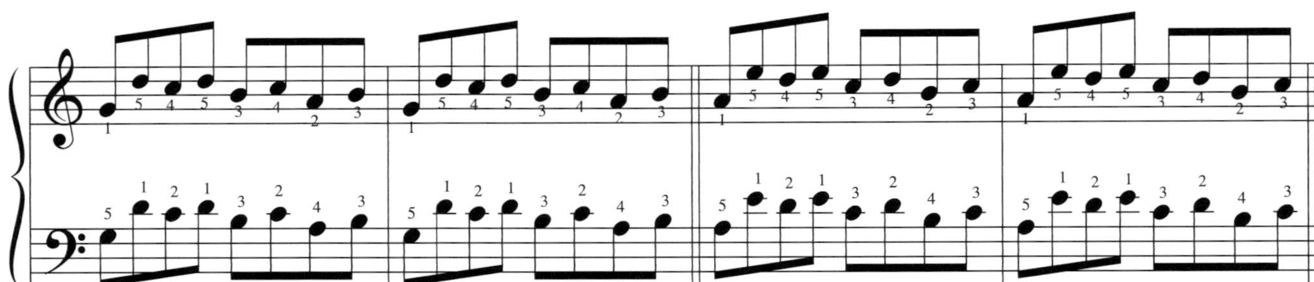

G hand position   A hand position

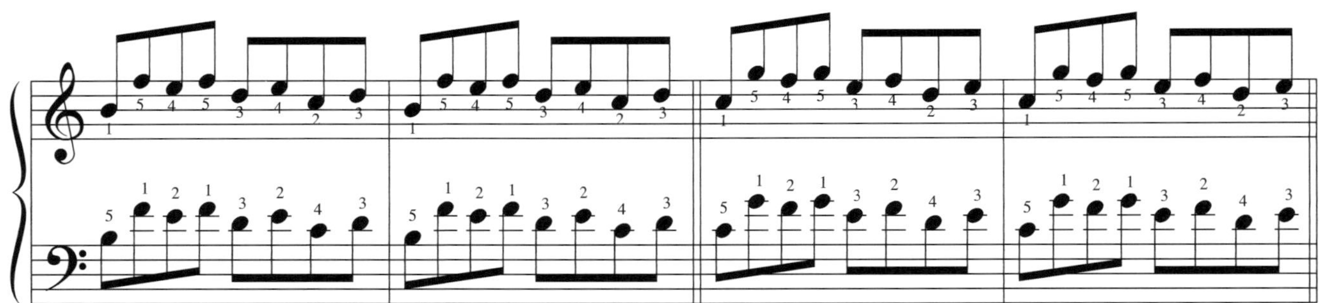

B hand position   C hand position

Exercise #3 Descending

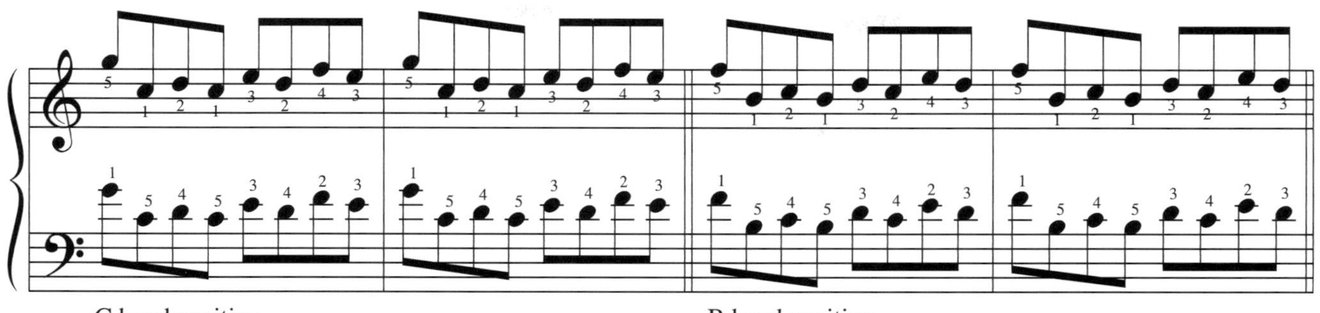

C hand position   B hand position

A hand position   G hand position

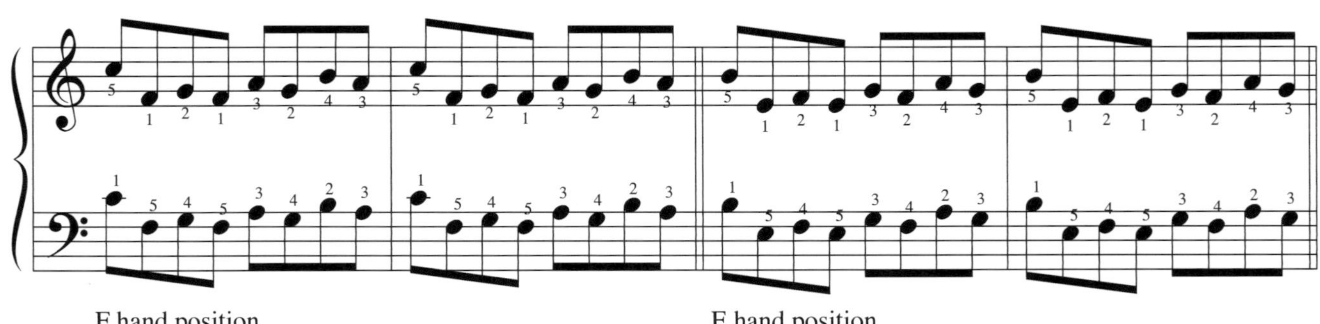

F hand position   E hand position

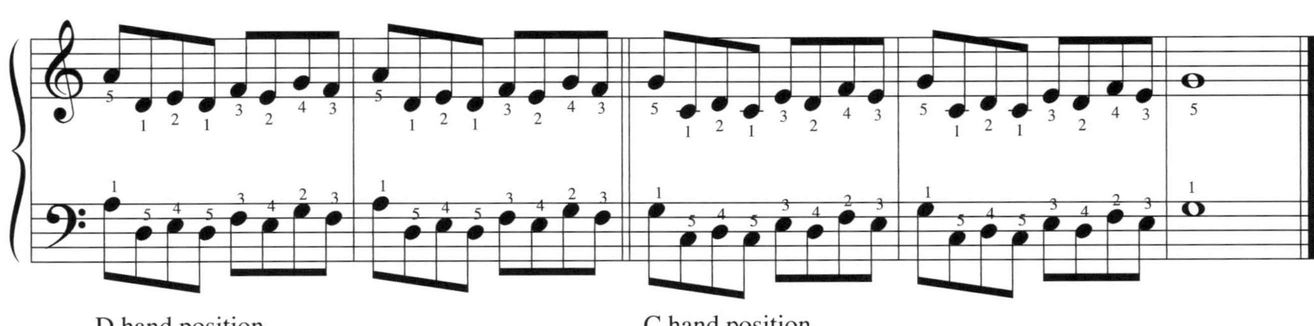

D hand position   C hand position

Exercise #4 Ascending

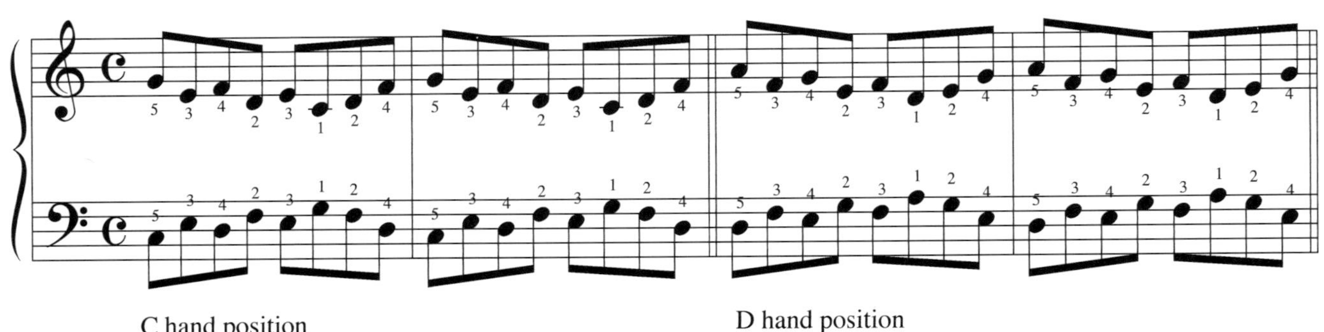

C hand position

D hand position

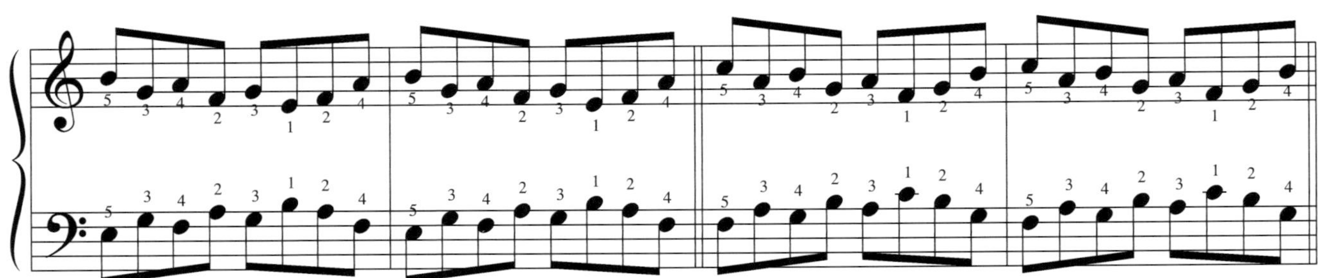

E hand position

F hand position

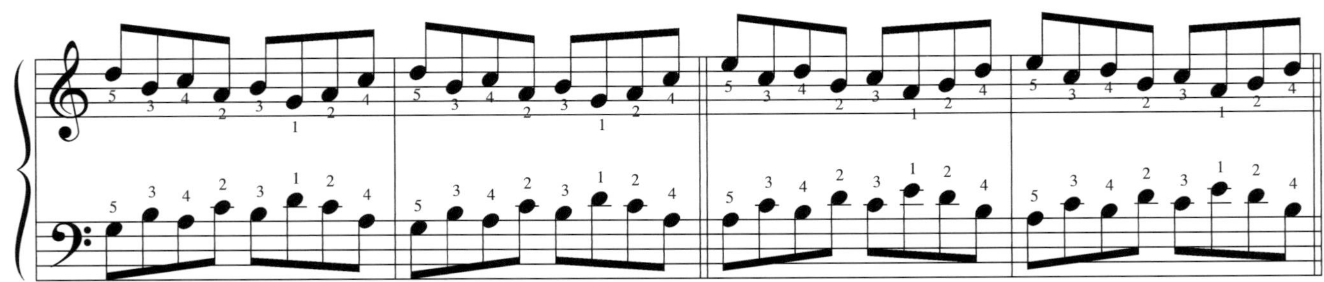

G hand position

A hand position

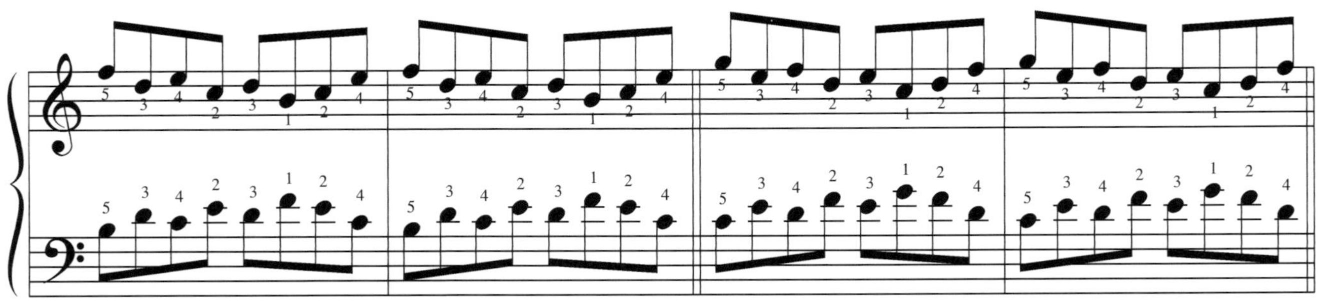

B hand position

C hand position

Exercise #4 Descending

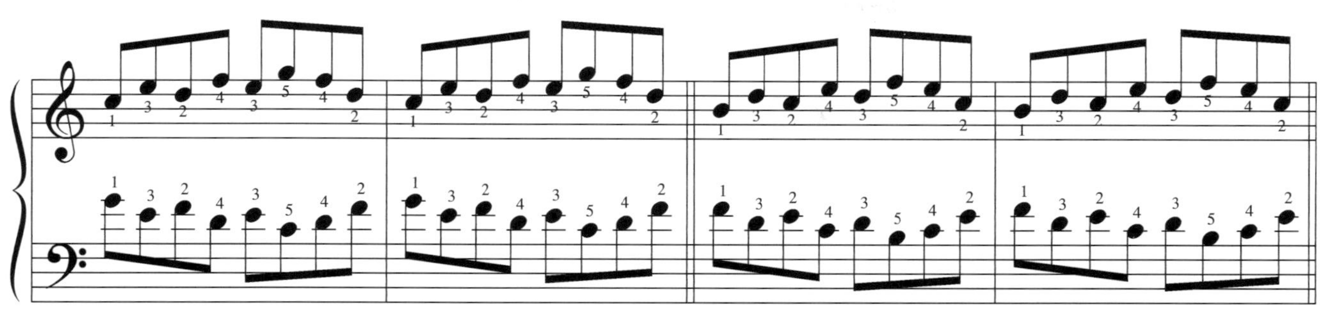

C hand position

B hand position

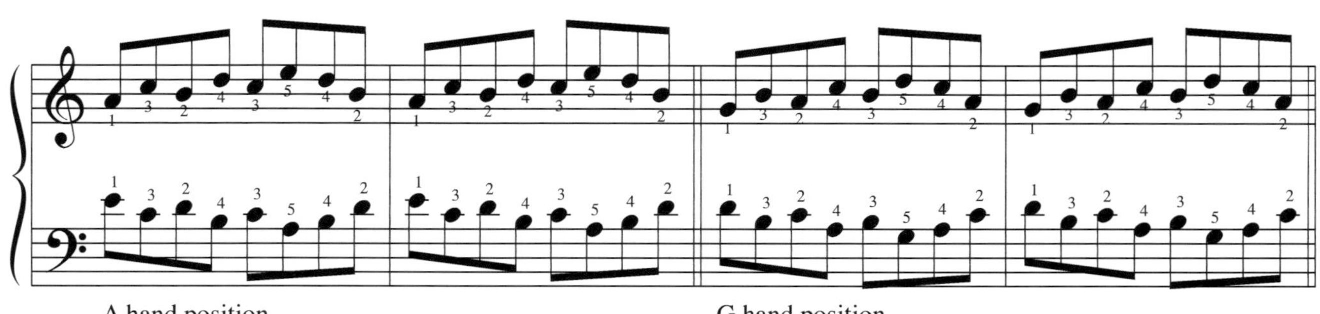

A hand position

G hand position

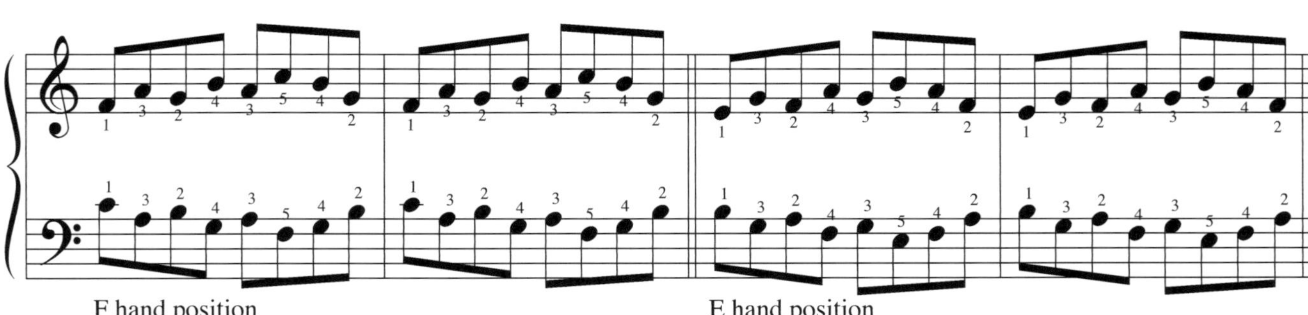

F hand position

E hand position

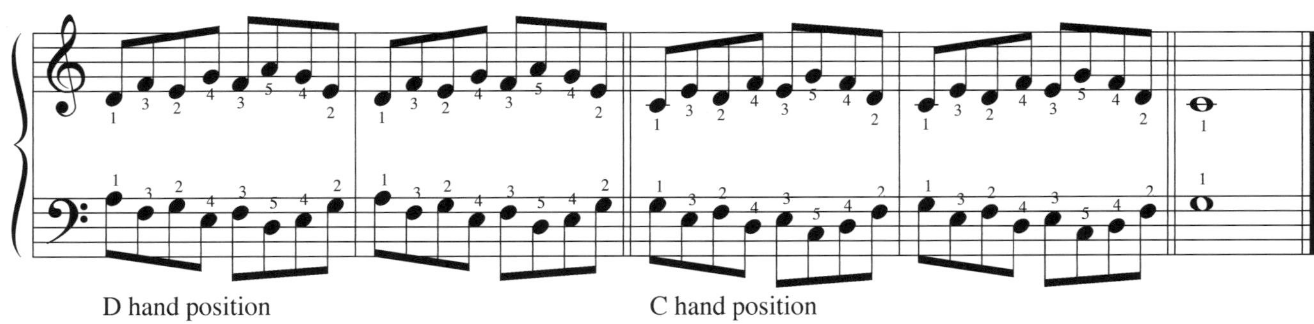

D hand position

C hand position

Appendix 1: Triads in a Scale; Inversions of Triads

Root position triads: C Major

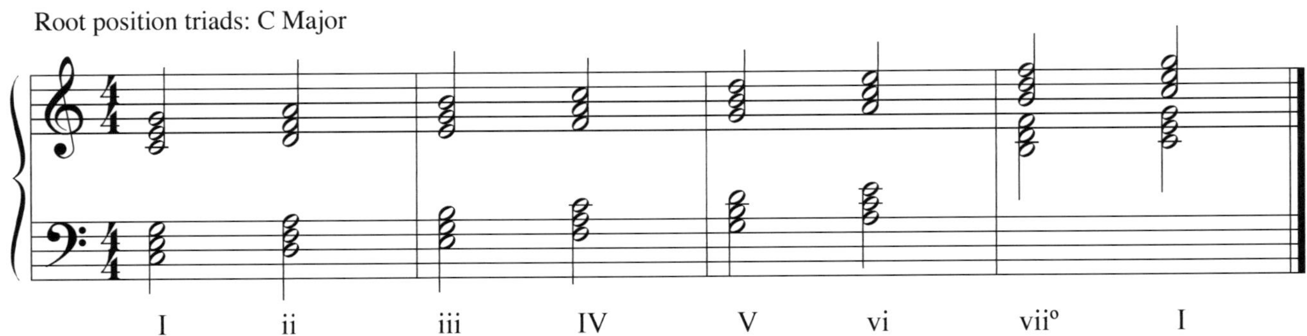

Inversions of primary triads: C Major

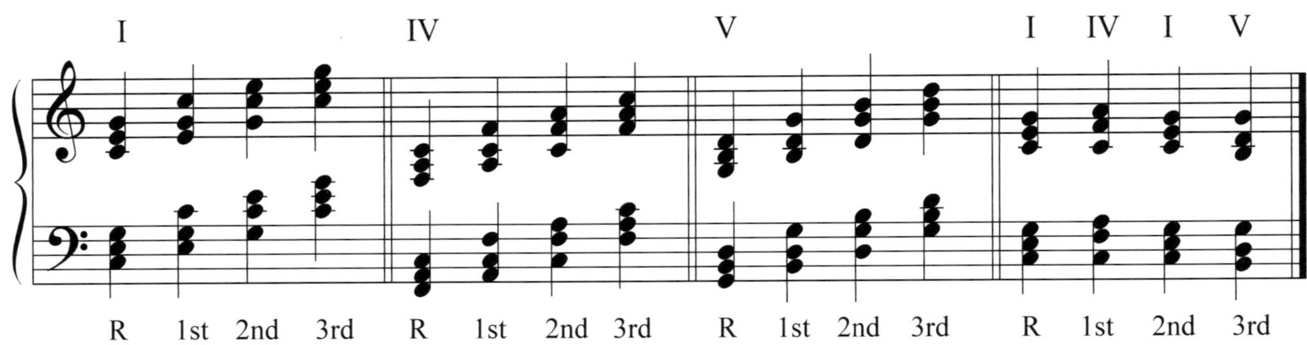

Root position triads: A minor

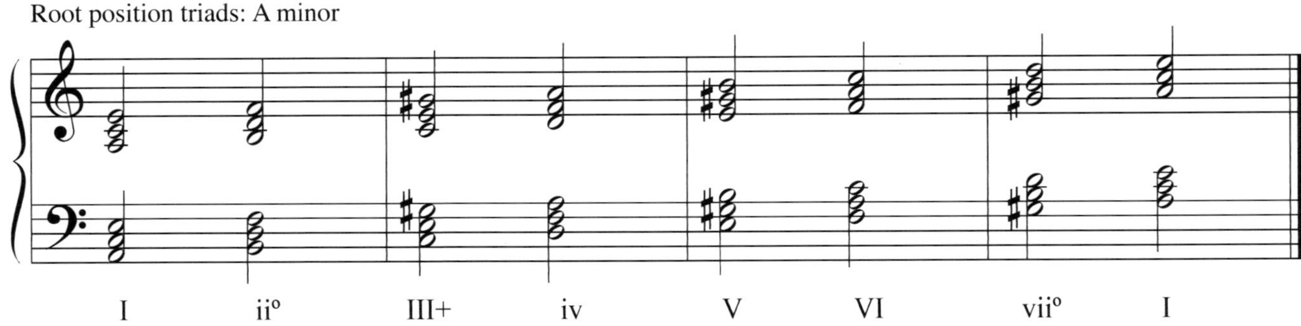

Inversions of primary triads: A minor

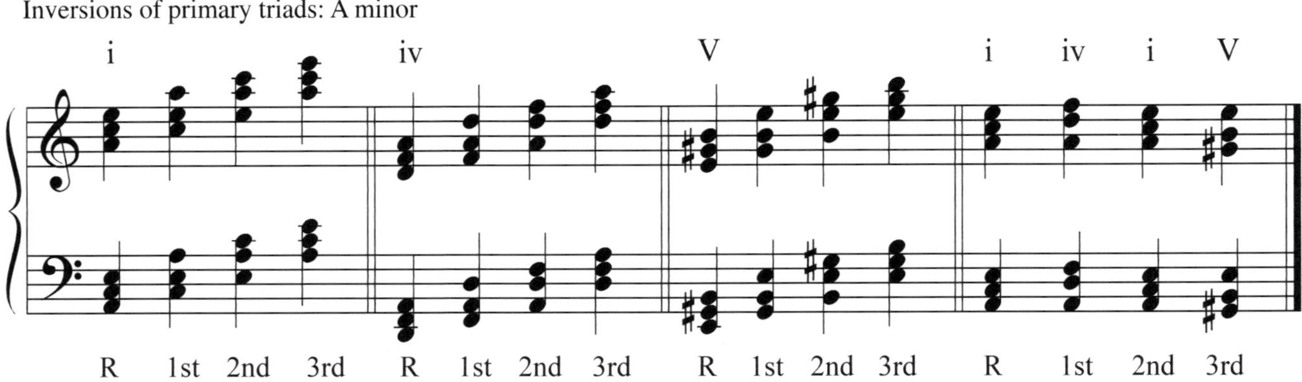

Appendix 1: Triads/inversions cont'd

Root position triads: F Major

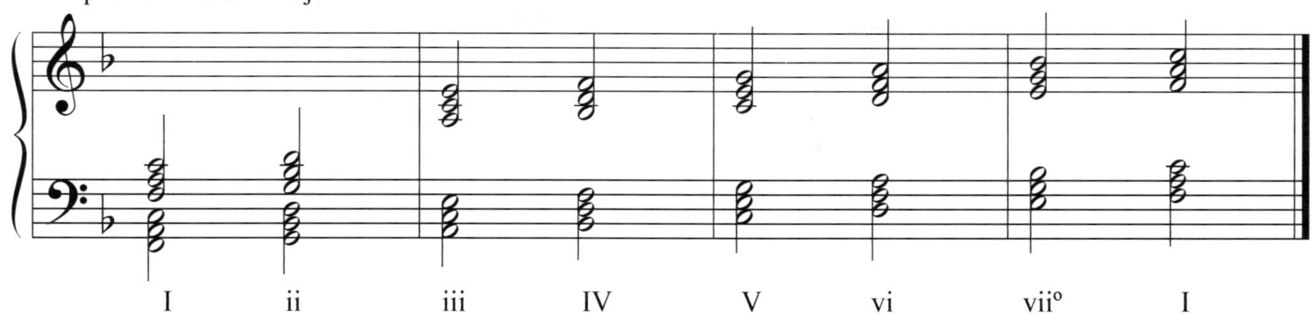

Inversions of primary triads: F Major

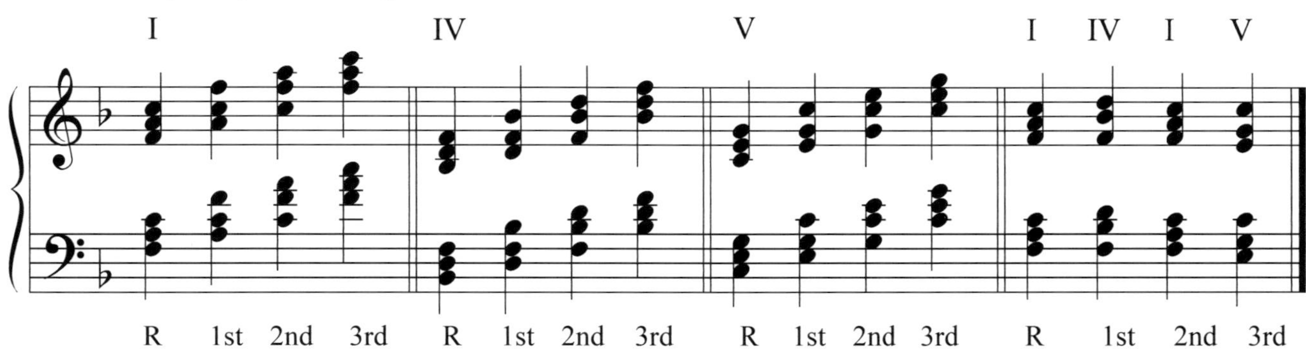

Root position triads: D minor

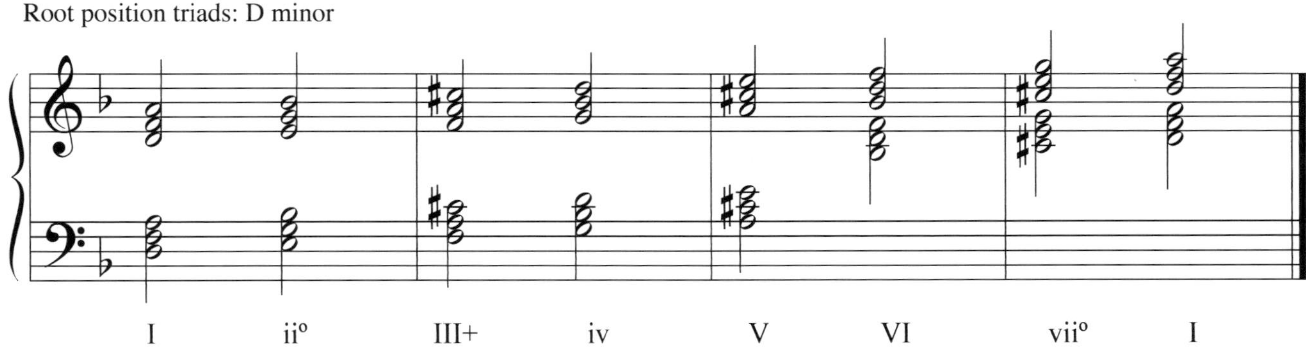

Inversions of primary triads: D minor

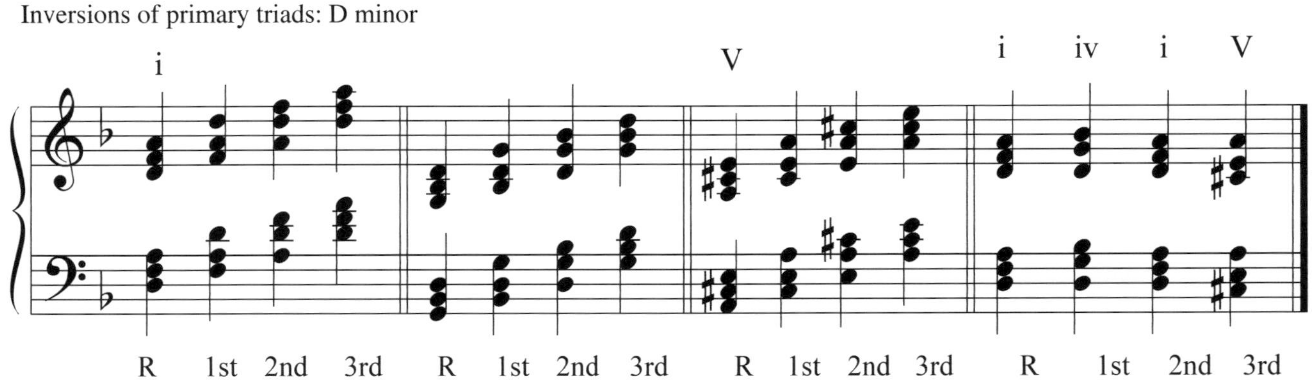

Appendix 1: Triads/inversions cont'd

Root position triads: G Major

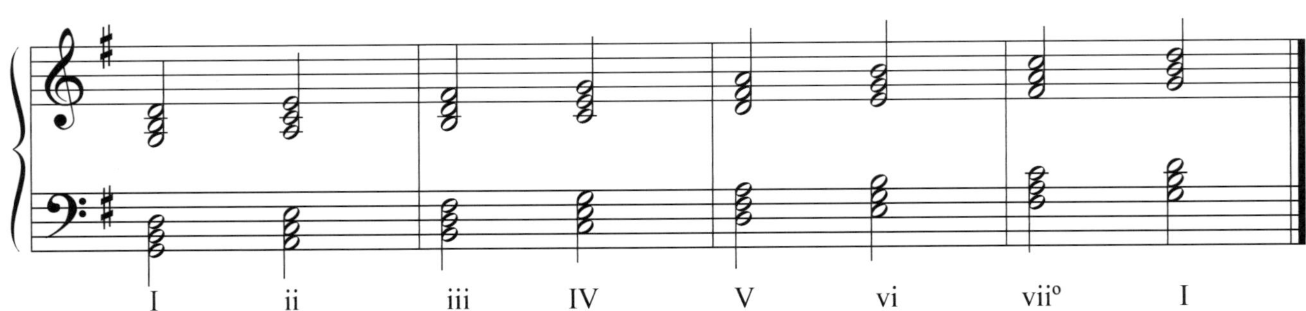

Inversions of primary triads: G Major

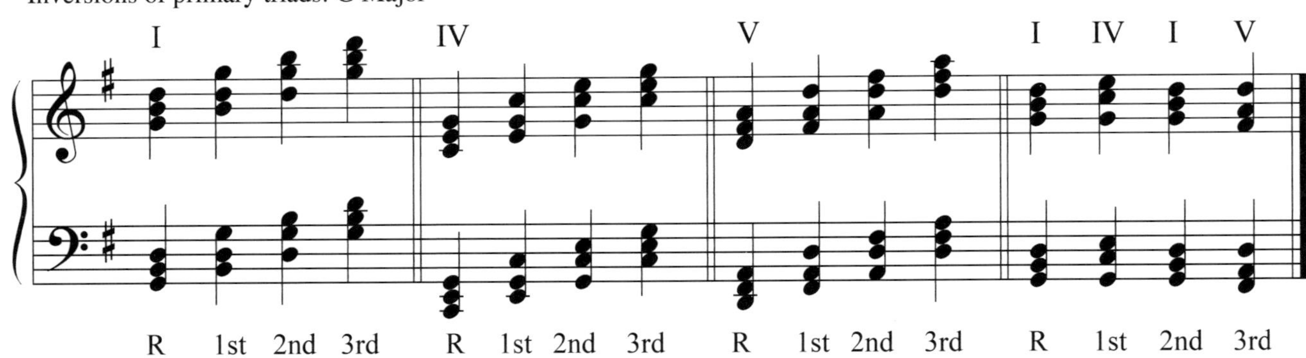

Root position triads: E minor

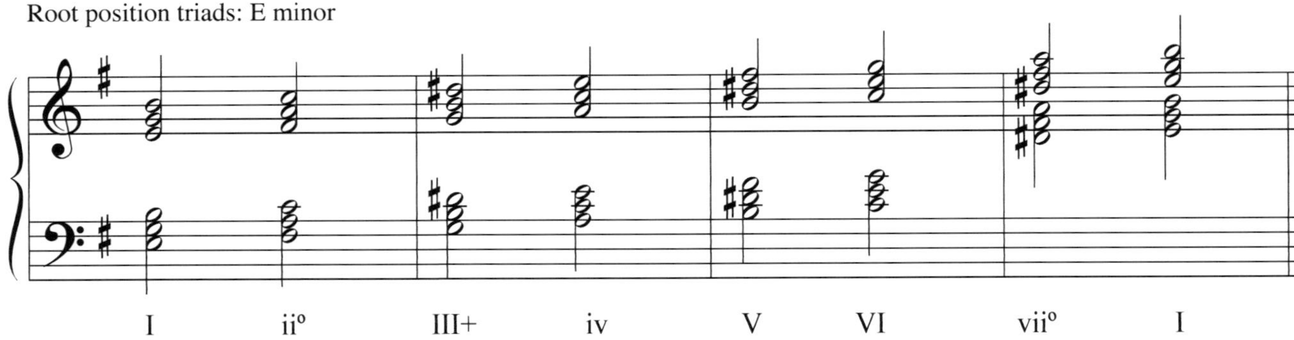

Inversions of primary triads: E minor

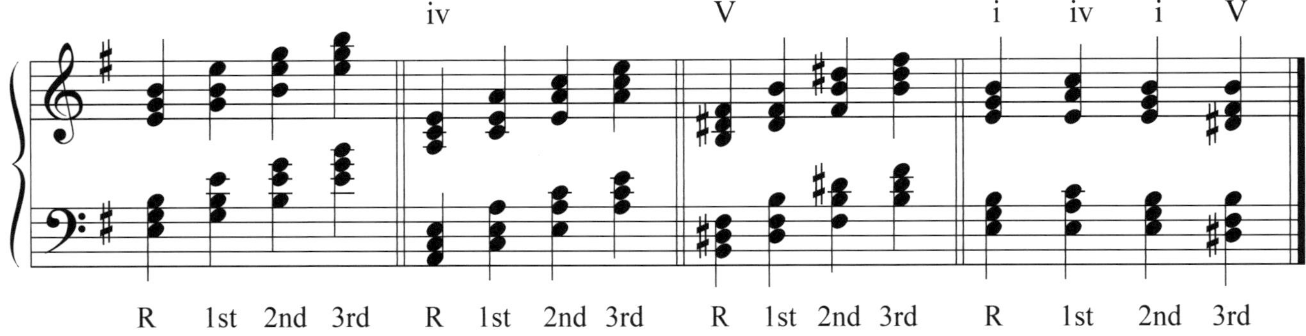

Appendix 1: Triads/inversions cont'd

Root position triads: D Major

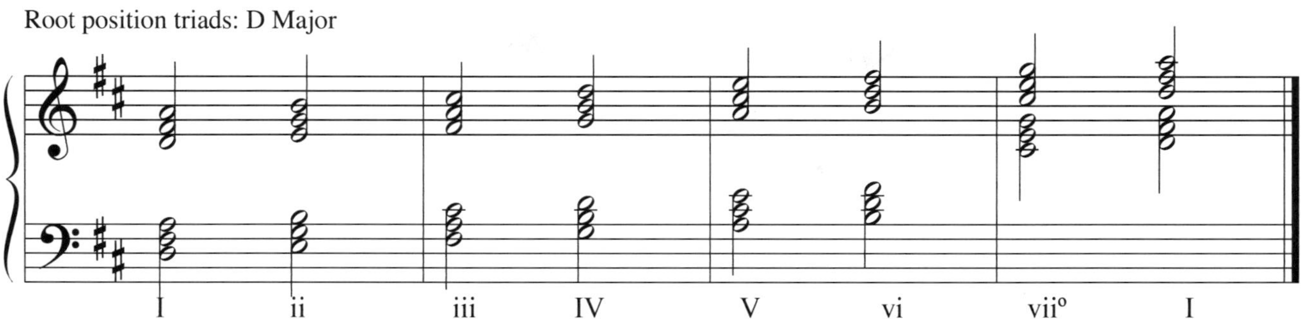

Inversions of primary triads: D Major

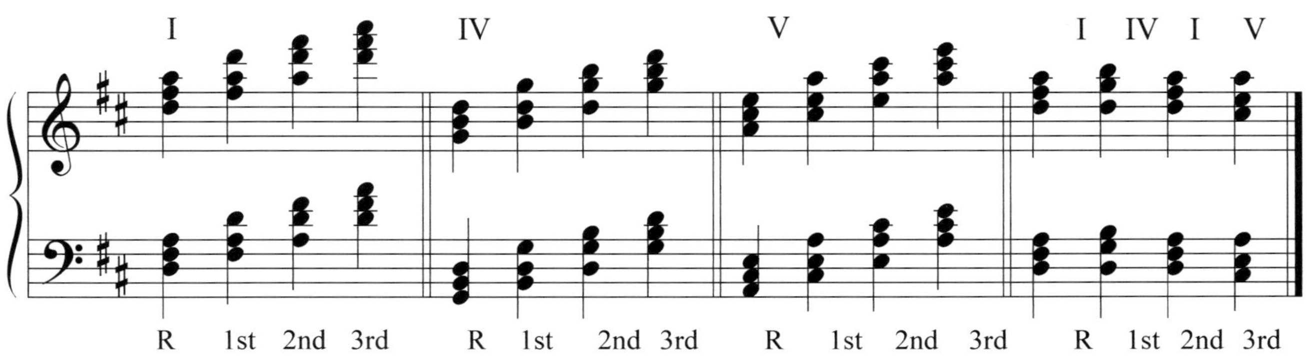

Root position triads: B minor

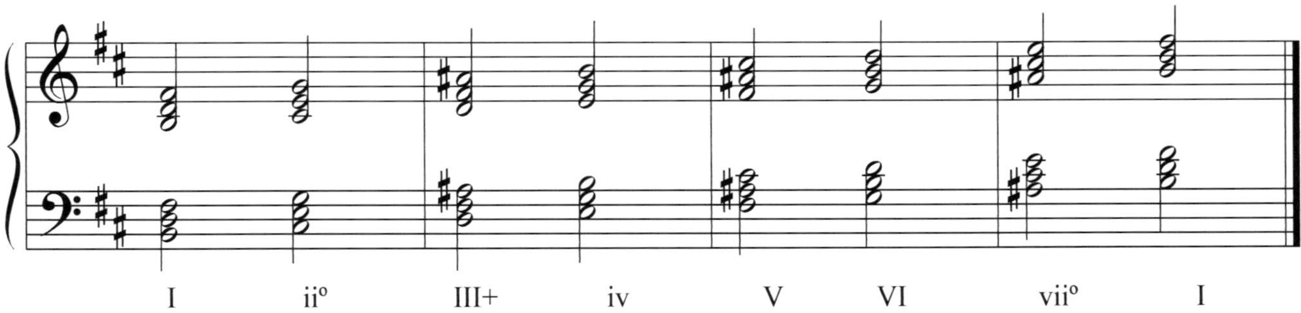

Inversions of primary triads: B minor

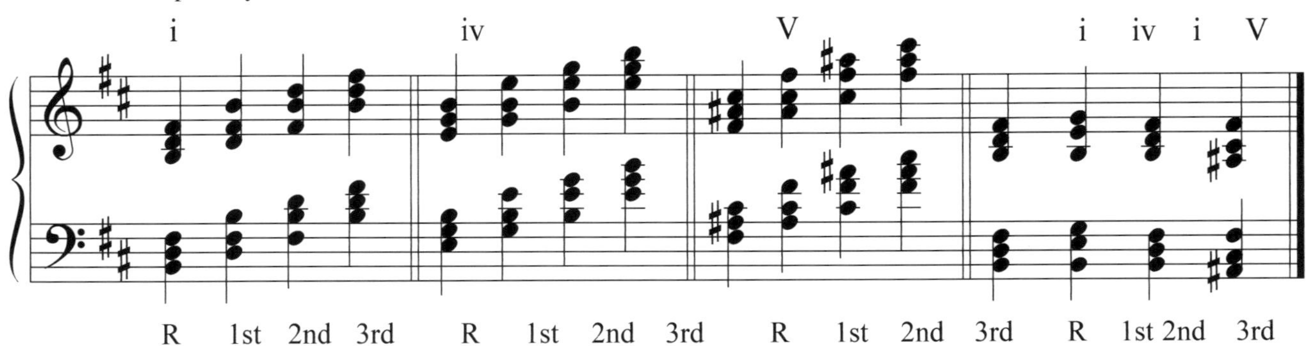

Appendix 1: Triads/inversions cont'd

Root position triads: B♭ Major

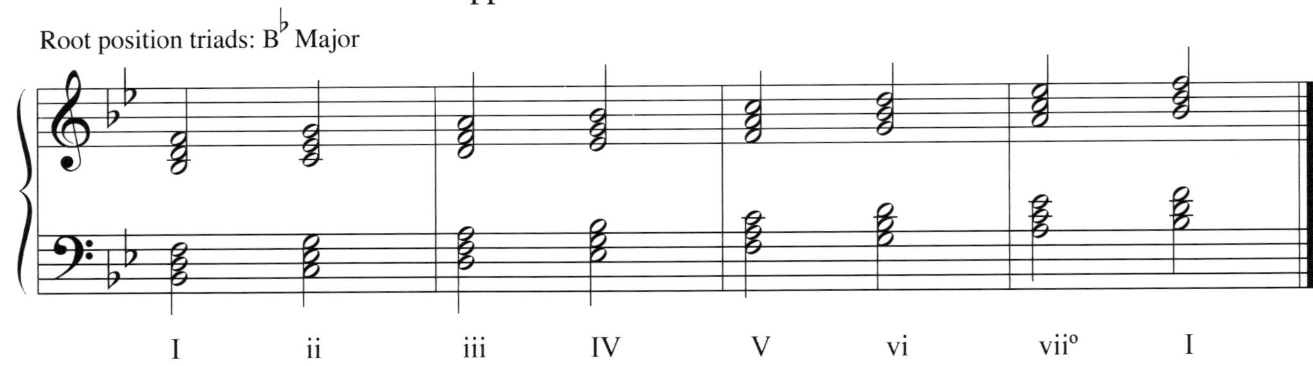

Inversions of primary triads: B♭ Major

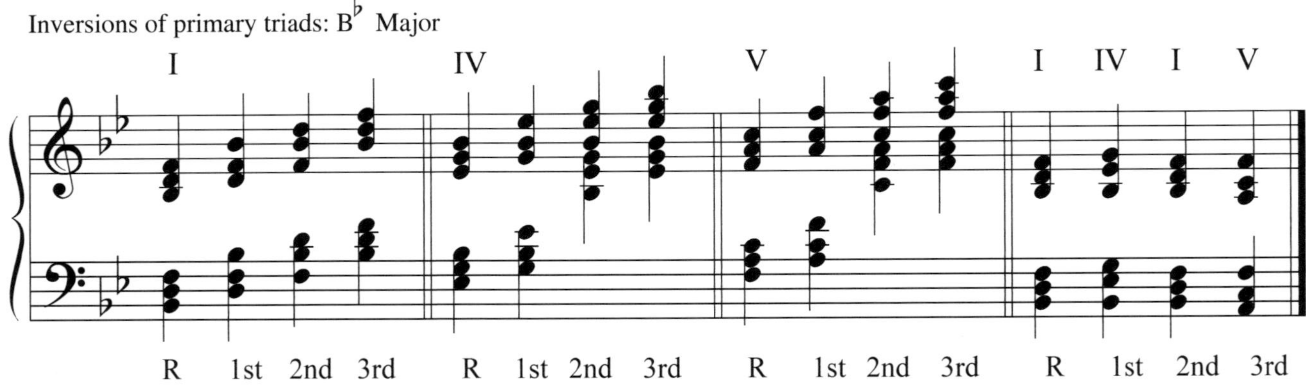

Root position triads: G minor

Inversions of primary triads: g harmonic minor

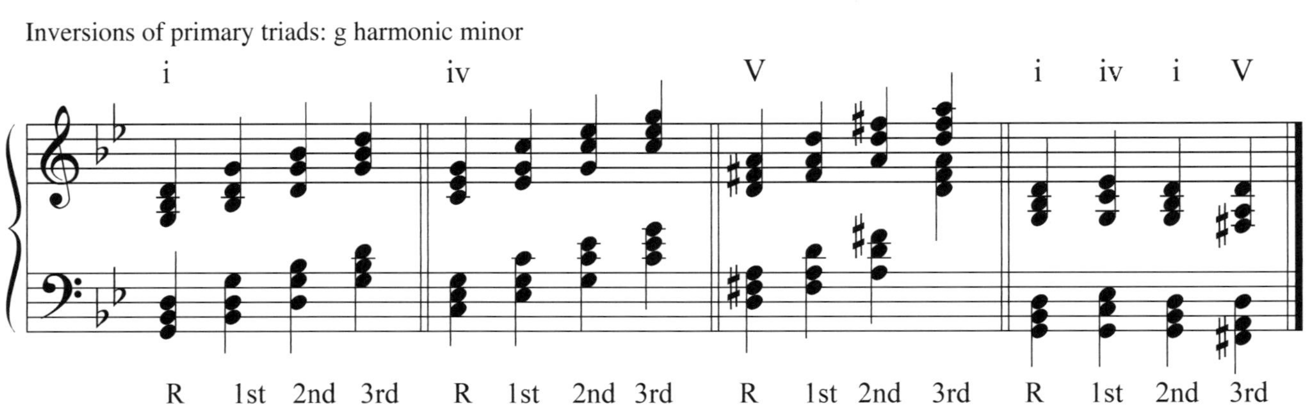

Appendix 2: Melodic Phrases

The material presented here is intended to supplement the harmonized melody and improvisation examples. "Melodic phrase" refers to the phrase construction found in simple common melodies such as popular music, folk tunes, hymn tunes and chorales. Although this material may apply to phrase construction found in larger classical music literature, generally the melodic phrase construction of art music is more complex and is beyond the scope of these materials.

Melodies are comprised of PHRASES. For example, the following melody consists of three phrases:

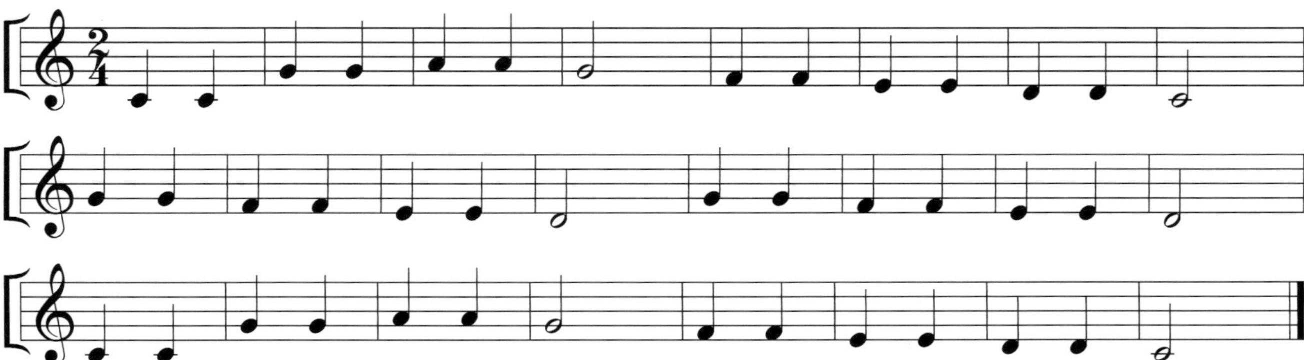

Here is a common definition of PHRASE:

A phrase is the SHORTest passage of music expressing a COMPLETE MUSICAL THOUGHT and ending in a CADENCE.*

There are three key points to this definition: (1) short, (2) complete musical thought, and (3) cadence. Hopefully, "short" will not need extensive elaboration. However, a common error in determining a phrase is getting it TOO short. More on this later.

COMPLETE MUSICAL THOUGHT means an instance of tension / relaxation. This duality is the basis of "complete musical thought" and is related to the same kind of duality present in classical poetic meters. In the above example, each phrase can easily be divided into its respective tension / relaxation (i.e., each phrase = 4 meas.; tension = 2 meas., relaxation = 2 meas.; half notes indicate points of division). Not all melodies are this obvious. However, a great number of successful melodies do consist of combinations of 4 or 8 measure phrases. With this explanation of "complete musical thought" in mind, examine the above melody again. It is easy to understand why some might make the mistake of defining the phrases in this melody as consisting of 2 measures instead of 4 measures. However, after playing or singing this example the tension / relaxation scenario should become apparent. This particular melody has three phrases and in that regard is not as common as many melodies which have 2 or 4 phrases.

In the above definition, "cadence" does not mean what it meant in an earlier section of this book -- a simple progression of block chords. Instead, CADENCE here means a point of relaxation of the tension at the end of the phrase. There are specific kinds of cadences and all phrases end with one of these specific cadences (see Appendix 3).

Analyze the melodies in the **Melodies for Harmonization** section of this book to determine their phrase construction. In addition to finding tension / relaxation, you might look for these often obvious characteristics of phrase construction:

- •. Sometimes the CADENCE POINT is the longest note value of the phrase. See examples #7, p. 40; #37, p. 47.

- • Often phrases consist of 4 or 8 measures (depending on the tempo), as in the example above.

* Definition based on Douglass Green's, *Form in Tonal Music*, 3rd edition, Harcourt Brace Jovanovich College Publisher, 1979.

Appendix 3: Melodic Cadences

As mentioned in **Appendix 2**, melodic phrases end with a cadence. In this sense, "cadence" refers to what happens at the end of a phrase and has nothing to do with the "block-chord" cadences (chord progressions) that you are required to learn in order to harmonize melodies and improvise. Here, CADENCE is a "point of rest" at the end of a phrase.

There are only TWO categories of cadences: (1) conclusive, and (2) inconclusive. All types of cadences fall into these two categories. A CONCLUSIVE CADENCE is a cadence on the I chord and an INCONCLUSIVE CADENCE is a cadence on a chord other than the I chord, for example the V chord.

Regarding CONCLUSIVE CADENCES, there are 2 types: (a) authentic, and (b) plagal. An AUTHENTIC CADENCE consists of 2 chords where the PENULTIMATE (next-to-last) chord contains a leading tone. Consequently, the most typical kind of AUTHENTIC CADENCE is V or V7 moving to I. In a PLAGAL CADENCE, the penultimate chord does not have a leading tone. The most typical kind of PLAGAL CADENCE is IV moving to the I chord. In an AUTHENTIC CADENCE, if the I chord is in root position and the tonic is in the melody (top most voice), then it is known as a "perfect authentic cadence."

INCONCLUSIVE CADENCES are not divided into types like conclusive cadences. There is only one type of inconclusive cadence -- those that cadence on a chord other than the I chord, for example the V chord. Another name for the inconclusive cadence is HALF CADENCE. It is important to know that a cadence on V is not the definition of "half cadence" but merely an EXAMPLE of a half cadence. Other half cadences could be cadences on IV ("Auld Lang Syne"), cadences on III ("I've been working on the rail road"), and cadences on vi (deceptive cadence). There is no such thing as a "perfect half cadence." PERFECT when applied to a cadence only refers to an authentic cadence.

To successfully harmonize a melody, it is important to have a step-by-step procedure rather than just willy-nilly sticking in chords. Here is a practical procedure for harmonizing a melody. If you use this you will have consistent success:

    1. Identify the phrases. Often phrases can be identified by counting 4 or 8 measures (the majority of common melodies in the western tradition have phrases constructed of 4 or 8 measures), looking for the longest note value (often the cadence point at the end of a phrase is the longest note value of the phrase), or by looking for some aspect of tension and relaxation (question/answer). See the melody below for reference.

    2. Harmonize the CADENCE POINTS first. The cadence point is the 2nd chord of the two-chord progression of the cadence, for example V7 - I. The V7 chord is the "penultimate chord" and the I chord is the "cadence point." Generally, there are only two possibilities to harmonize the cadence point: I or V. Remember (from above), there are ONLY TWO categories of cadences: conclusive and non conclusive. So, once you identify the cadence points at the ends of the various phrases it should be relatively easy to determine if the cadence points are I or V. If the cadence point is a V, then it is better to cadence on V rather than V7 (although for Level I piano, the V chord voicing is not presented so it is OK to cadence on V7 rather than V).

    3. Next, harmonize the PENULTIMATE CHORD -- that is, the chord right before the cadence point. If the cadence point is the I chord, then you have two possibilities: (a) V7 - I, or (b) IV - I. In the first case that would be an authentic cadence and in the second case it would be a plagal cadence. It most cases it simply doesn't matter which possibility you use. If the cadence point is not a I chord (it's going to be an inconclusive cadence), then your 1st choice should be the V chord since BY FAR this is the most common inconclusive (half) cadence. Yes, there are rare example where a IV chord or a III chord would work, but your BEST CHOICE would simply be to use the V chord. Do not cadence on a ii chord. If you feel the chord HAS to be the ii chord, then chances are you are trying to harmonize the "tension" part of the phrase (as in, tension/relaxation) and you have not really found the true cadence point of the phrase.

    4. Harmonize the rest of the melody. Now that you have the cadences at the ends of the phrases harmonized, go ahead and harmonize the rest of the melody using the suggested harmonic rhythm. From here on out, the harmonization procedure will be relative straight forward: if the melody note is in the chord you are trying to use, then IT WILL WORK. There are some simple guidelines to use: (a) often the melody notes will outline specific chords and this will be a good

Material based on Douglass Green's, *Form in Tonal Music*, 3rd edition, Harcourt Brace Jovanovich College Publisher, 1979.

clue as to what chord to use, (b) it's OK to use the same chord consecutively -- you don't have to change chords on every instances of the harmonic rhythm, (c) V7-I used within the phrase works best when the I chord is on a strong beat and the V7 chord is on a weak beat. This is not a hard and fast rule, but it generally works well.

Here is an example:

Find the phrases, identify and then harmonize the cadence points. How many phrases does this tune have?

-- The answer is TWO PHRASES. Count 8 measure phrases and look for the LONGEST note values.
-- The longest note values ARE the CADENCE POINTS, and you should be able to see that there are 2 phrases.
-- There is an aspect of TENSION from the beginning through the 2nd beat of meas. 4. This is followed by a
    RELAXATION from the 3rd beat of meas. 4 through the cadence point of meas. 8 and 9. A similar structure
    can be found from the 3rd beat of meas. 9 through the 2nd cadence point at the end of the tune.
-- The first cadence point should be harmonized by the V chord (or V7, if Level Preparatory or Level I).
-- The second cadence point should be harmonized by the I chord.

-- The 1st cadence is an inconclusive cadence (half cadence}; the second cadence is a conclusive (authentic)
    cadence.

Continue harmonizing the rest of the tune. Keep it SIMPLE. It's OK to use the same chord consecutively, especially if the melody outlines specific chords. Keep in mind the HARMONIC RHYTHM, in this case -- one dotted half note for each measure. Notice how the first phrase cadences on a V chord and then moves to a V7 chord. This creates a stronger cadence than just cadencing on the V7 chord. Although, for Preparatory and Level I piano this will not be an option.

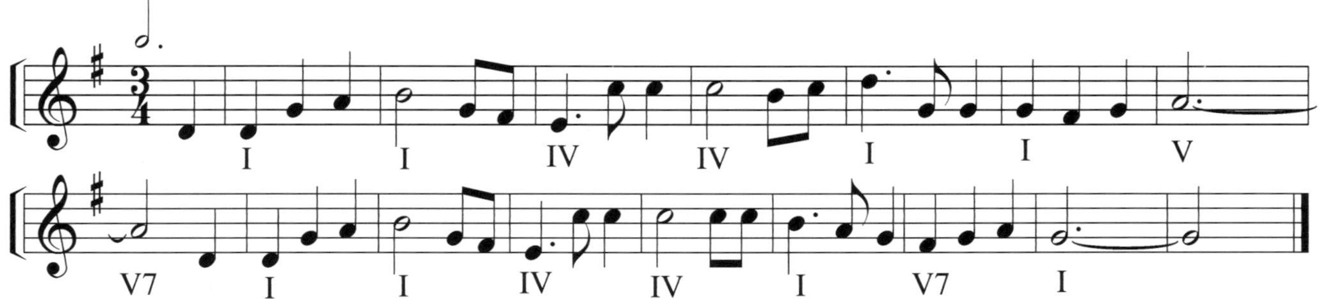

Appendix 4: Non-Chord Tones

A NON-CHORD TONE is a note in a melody which is not part of the chord or harmony which is being used for harmonization at the point where the NON-CHORD TONE appears. Generally, there are two types of NON-CHORD TONES:

1. Unaccented (occurs on a weak beat or a weak part of a beat)
2. Accented (occurs on a strong beat)

The terms "accented" and "unaccented" are subjective because the "feel" of accented/unaccented depends on such factors as tempo and harmonic rhythm.

Here are some examples of NON-CHORD TONES . The numbers indicate different NON-CHORD TONES which are explained below:

1. PASSING TONE. One of the most common non-chord tones, the PASSING TONE "passes" between two adjacent chord tones. "Adjacent" means the next chord tone, either up or down. In the chord, C-E-G, "E" and "G" are adjacent but "C" and "G" are nonadjacent. So the PASSING TONE between C-E would be "D". The PASSING TONE between E-G would be F.

2. NEIGHBOR TONE. Also one of the most common-chord tones, the NEIGHBOR TONE is a diatonic step UP or DOWN from any chord tone. If the NEIGHBOR TONE is above the chord-tone then it's an "UPPER NEIGHBOR TONE." And if it's below, its called a LOWER NEIGHBOR TONE. The example above (#2) is a LOWER NEIGHBOR TONE.

3. ACCENTED PASSING TONE. If a passing tone occurs on a strong beat then it's called an ACCENTED PASSING TONE. Notice that the note before and after are chord-tones.

4. ANTICIPATION. An ANTICIPATION, "anticipates" the upcoming chord. So, this implies that at least TWO chords and 3 melody notes are involved. The 1st note is a chord tone associated with the 1st chord and the 2nd note (which is the actual ANTICIPATION) is a non-chord tone associated with the 2nd chord. In the example above (#4), the "E" is a chord-tone and is associated with the C major triad on beat 1. The "F" on beat 2 is not part of the C major triad but is a part of the F major triad on beat 3. An ANTICIPATION always occurs on a weak beat.

5. SUSPENSION. A SUSPENSION is the similar to an ANTICIPATION except that it always occurs on a STRONG beat. It must have TWO chords involved and THREE melody notes. The 1st melody note is associated with the 1st chord and occurs on a WEAK beat. The 2nd melody note is THE SAME as the 1st melody note but is associated with the second chord and occurs on a strong beat. This 2nd melody note is the actual SUSPENSION and it's a NON-CHORD TONE (not part of the 2nd chord). The 3rd melody note "resolves" to a chord tone in the 2nd chord.

6. APPOGGIATURA. An APPOGGIATURA is a type of ACCENTED non-chord tone and is very similar to a SUSPENSION: it must have TWO chords involved and THREE melody notes. Here's the difference: the 2nd melody note is DIFFERENT from the 1st melody note and it SKIPS to a non-chord tone associated with the 2nd chord and then "resolves" BY STEP in the OPPOSITE DIRECTION from the skip. If this seems complex, then just study the example. Some music theorists consider all ACCENTED non-chord tones to be APPOGGIATURAS. See "appoggiatura" in *Harvard's Dictionary of Music.*

7. ESCAPE TONE. An ESCAPE TONE occurs on a WEAK beat and consists of a step (either up or down) followed by a skip in the opposite direction to a CHORD TONE in either the same chord or a different chord.

There are other NON-CHORD TONES but they will not be discussed here. You will no doubt cover them in your theory courses.

A question that is often asked by beginning theory students is, "Good grief! Why does all this matter?" Here's a simple answer:

Music theory is the SCIENCE of music. In any scientific field, one endeavors is to CLASSIFY all possible phenomena. For example, in the field of geology, one endeavors to classify all rocks and all phenomena concerning rocks. The same is true in ornithology, entomology, astronomy, physics, etc. The study of music is no different. To UNDERSTAND music at a deep level, one has to classify and NAME all possible musical phenomena. Although this may seem tedious and unimportant to the novice, it is invaluable to the professional musician.

Weekly Assignment Schedule

Week 1: Welcome to class
Prepare to take a written quiz <u>next class period</u> on Group I Scales (p. 64), <u>written material only</u>. The quiz will cover:
1. What scales are in this group?
2. What are the thumb notes of each scale?
3. What are the characteristics of the scales in this group?

Week 2: Repertory; Scales; Cadences; Harmonized Melodies; Exercises
- *Bagpipes*, p. 16
- Scales: D-flat major ; G-flat major, pp. 64- 65
- Cadence in C Major, p. 34
- Harmonized melodies:
  • Study the **Procedures for Harmonized Melodies**, p. 36-37
  • Take a <u>written quiz</u> in the next session (Week 3) on the **Procedures for Harmonized Melodies**, p. 36-37
- Exercise #1, play up one octave, p. 72

Week 3: Repertory; Scales; Cadences; Harmonized Melodies; Sight Reading; Exercises
- *Folk Song*, p. 17
- Scales: B-flat natural minor ; E-flat natural minor, pp. 64; 66
- Cadences: all major keys, p. 34
- Harmonized melodies: Study and practice the Accompaniment Patterns on p. 35. Play any on request.
- Sight Read p. 50
- Exercise #1, up one and down octave, pp. 72-73

Week 4: Repertory; Scales; Cadences; Harmonized Melodies; Sight Reading; Exercises
- *Minuet in F*, p. 19
- Scales: B-flat harmonic minor ; E-flat harmonic minor, pp. 64; 67
- Cadences: review all major keys, p. 34
- Harmonized melodies: Harmonize melody #22, p. 42 using block chords and an accompaniment pattern (p. 35)
- Sight Read p. 51
- Exercise #1, up one and down octave, pp. 72-73

Week 5: Repertory; Scales; Cadences; Triads; Sight Reading; Exercises
- *Minuet in C* p. 20
- Scales: B Major, pp. 64- 65
- Cadences: review all major keys, p. 34
- Triads: Play Major and minor triads (without using the music) on each white note C-B, p. 32
- Sight Read p. 52
- Exercise #1, up one and down octave, pp. 72-73

Week 6: Repertory; Scales; Cadences; Triads; Sight Reading; Exercises
- *Peasant Song*, p. 23 -- Not due for a grade this week; get started on it.
- Scales: B natural minor; B harmonic minor, pp. 64; 66-67
- Cadences: review all major keys, p. 34
- Triads: Review Major and minor triads on each white note C-B, p. 32 (play them without using the music)
- Sight Read p. 53
- Exercise #1, up one and down octave, pp. 72-73

Week 7: Repertory; Scales; Cadences; Improvisation; Triads; Sight Reading; Exercises
- *Peasant Song*, p. 23
- Scales: F Major scale, pp. 64- 65
- Cadences: All minor cadences in, p. 34
- Improvisation: Study the written material on pp. 44-45.
- More Improvisation -- compose RHYTHMIC MOTIVES for the examples on p. 46:
    • create four rhythmic motives for each meter
    • write out the motives (using whatever notes you like), a DIFFERENT motive for each measure
    • you will use these motives for all subsequent improvisations
- Sight Read p. 54
- Exercise #1, up one and down octave, pp. 72-73

Week 8: Repertory; Scales; Cadences; Harmonized Melodies; Sight Reading; Exercises
- Repertory: No repertory due this week, but get started on *Uncle Willie...*, p. 24 which will be due next week.
- Scales: F natural minor scale; F harmonic minor scale, pp. 64; 66-67
- Cadences: Review all minor cadences in, p. 34
- Review Procedures for Harmonization, p. 36 - 37
- Harmonized Melodies: Harmonize melody #4, p. 38 (A minor); melody #6, p. 39 (E minor)
    • Use block chords to harmonize your melodies
    • Be able to play one of the melodies using one of the Accompaniment Patterns, p. 35.
- Sight Read p. 55
- Exercise #1, up one and down octave; Exercise #2, up one octave pp. 72-74

Week 9: Repertory; Scales; Cadences; Improvisation; Sight Reading; Exercises
- *Uncle Willie...*, p. 24
- Scales: Review all major scales to date: D-flat; G-flat; B; F, pp. 64- 65
- Cadences: Review all minor cadences, p. 34
- Improvisation: Using the rhythmic motives you composed on p. 46, improvise melodies to examples on the
    bottom of p. 46 and the top of p. 47:
    • don't write out your improvisation
    • use the same rhythmic motive for each measure except at the cadence points
    • use a LONG NOTE (whole note; dotted whole note) at the cadence points
- Sight Read pp. 50-55
- Exercise #1 and #2 complete, pp. 72-75

Week 10: Repertory; Scales; Cadences; Harmonized Melodies; Sight Reading; Exercises
- Repertory: No repertory this week, but get started on *What Wondrous...*, p. 26 which will be due next week.
- Scales: Review all natural minor scales to date: b-flat; e-flat; b; f, pp. 64, 66
- Cadences: Review all Major and minor cadences, p. 34
- Harmonize Melody #17, p. 41 (B-flat Major)
- Improvisation: Example #1 on page 48 -- a CHORD PROGRESSION. Follow the procedures written above
    the chord progressions.
- Sight Read p. 54, each part separately
- Exercise #1 and #2 complete, pp. 72-75

Week 11: Repertory; Scales; Cadences; Triads; Sight Reading; Exercises
- *What Wondrous Love...*, p. 26
- Scales: Review all harmonic minor scales to date: b-flat; e-flat; b; f, pp. 64; 67
- Cadences: Review all Major and minor cadences, p. 34
- Triads: Review all Major and minor triads, pp. 32-33
- Sight Read pp. 50-55
- Exercise #1 and #2 complete, pp. 72-75

Week 12: Repertory; Scales; Triads; Cadences; Improvisation; Sight Reading; Exercises
- Repertory: No repertory this week, but get started on *Revenge of Debbie*, p. 28 which will be due next week.
- Repertory: Also get started on *Capriccio*, p. 31.
  • This piece (*Capriccio*) will be due for a grade on Week 15.
  • You will have to MEMORIZE this piece (*Capriccio*) and play it as part of a FINAL EXAM*
- Scales: All Scales, pp. 64- 67
- Cadences: Review all minor Cadences: A minor, D minor, E minor, p. 34
- Triads: Review all minor Triads: A minor, D minor, E minor, p. 32-33
- Improvisation: Do Improvisation Example #2, p. 48. Follow the procedures written above the chord progressions.
- Sight Read pp. 8-9
- Exercise #1 and #2 complete, pp. 72-75

  Please READ THIS: A memorized repertory piece will be required for your final exam. Ask your instructor for details.

Week 13: Repertory; Scales; Triads; Cadences; Harmonized melody; Sight Reading; Exercises
- Repertory: *The Revenge of Debbie*, p. 28. Play it for a grade this week.
- Repertory: Continue working on *Capriccio*, p. 31.
  • This piece (*Capriccio*) will be due for a grade on Week 15.
  • You will have to MEMORIZE this piece (*Capriccio*) and play it as part of a FINAL EXAM.*
- Scales: All Scales, pp. 64- 67
- Triads: All Triads, p. 32-33
- Cadences: All Cadences, p. 34
- Harmonized Melodies: Harmonize melody # 18, p. 41
- Sight Read p. 12
- Exercise #1 and #2 complete, pp. 72-75

Week 14: Repertory; Scales; Triads; Cadences; Improvisation; Sight Reading; Exercises
- Repertory: No repertory due this week. However, *Capriccio* (p. 31) will be due for a grade next week.
  • You will have to MEMORIZE *Capriccio* and play it as part of a FINAL EXAM.*
- All Scales, pp. 64- 67
- Triads: All Triads, p. 32-33
- Cadences: All Cadences, p. 34
- Improvisation: Do Improvisation Example #3, p. 48. Follow the procedures written above the chords progressions.
- Sight Read p. 13
- Exercise #1 and #2 complete, pp. 72-75

Week 15: Repertory; Scales; Exercises; Triads; Cadences; Harmonized Melodies; Improvisation; Sight Reading
- Repertory: *Capriccio*, p. 31 (from memory unless your instructor has told you otherwise)
- Have all the following material prepared. Your instructor may hear any of it for this week's assignment:
  • All Scales, pp. 64- 67
  • All Triads, p. 32-33
  • All Cadences, p. 34
  • All Exercises, , pp. 72-75
- Harmonize ANY (just one) of the melodies on pp. 42-43
- Improvisation: Do Improvisation Example #4, p. 48. Follow the procedures written above the chord progressions.
- Be prepared to Sight Read any example given to you by your instructor.

*A Final Exam may be arranged by the Instructor.

Class Notes

Class Notes

Level One Assignments

WK #	SCALES	REPERTORY	SIGHT READING	CADENCES	HARM. MEL	IMPROV	TRIADS	EXERCISES
1	Quiz on Group I & II Scales -- written material only, p. 64							
2	$D^\flat$, $G^\flat$	p. 16 *Bagpipes*		p. 34 C Major	p. 36-37 Procedures			p. 72 #1
3	$b^\flat$, $e^\flat$ natural only	p. 17 *Folk song*	p. 50	p. 34 All Maj keys	p. 37 Patterns			p. 72 #1
4	$e^\flat$, $b^\flat$ harmonic only	p. 19 *Minuet in F*	p. 51	p. 34 All Maj keys	p. 42 No. 22			p. 72 # 1
5	B	p. 20 *Minuet in C*	p. 52	p. 34 All Maj keys			See detail on p. 90	p. 72 #1
6	b nat & har	[p. 23 *Peasant Song*] See detail p. 90	p. 53	p. 34 All Maj keys			See detail on p. 90	p. 72 #1
7	F	p. 23 *Peasant Song*	p. 54	p. 34 All min keys		See detail on p. 91		p. 72 #1
8	f nat & har	[p. 24 *Uncle Willie*] See detail, p. 91	p. 55	p. 34 All min keys	p. 38 #4 p. 39 #6			p. 72-74 #1 & #2
9	review all majors todate	p. 24 *Uncle Willie*	pp. 50-55	p. 34 All min keys		See detail on p. 91		p. 72-75 #1 & #2
10	review all nat mins todate	[p. 26 *WondrousLove*] See detail, p. 91	pp. 50-55	p. 34 All keys	p. 41 No. 17	p. 48 No. 1		p. 72-75 #1 & #2
11	review all har mins todate	p. 26 *Wondrous Love*	pp. 50-55	p. 34 All keys			See detail on p. 91	p. 72-75 #1 & #2
12	review all scales todate	[p. 28 *Revenge of Debbie*] See detail p. 92	pp. 8-9	p. 34 All keys		p. 48 No. 2	See detail on p. 91	p. 72-75 #1 & #2
13	review all scales todate	p. 28 *Revenge of Debbie*	p. 12	p. 34 All keys	p. 41 No. 18		See detail on p. 92	p. 72-75 #1 & #2
14	review all scales todate	[p. 31 *Capriccio*] See detail, p. 92	p. 13	p. 34 All keys		p. 48 No. 3	See detail on p. 92	p. 72-75 #1 & #2
15	All scales todate	p. 31 *Capriccio*	See detail on p. 92	p. 34 All keys	Choose any on pp. 42-43	p. 48 No. 4	See detail on p. 92	p. 72-75 #1 & #2

All scales,, cadences, triads, and exercises should be performed from memory when playing for a grade. Failure to do so will result in a lowered grade.

The repertory piece for Week 15 should be played from memory unless your instructor indicates otherwise.